OFFICE-HOLDERS IN MODERN BRITAIN

V

Home Office Officials

1782–1870

OFFICE-HOLDERS
IN MODERN BRITAIN

V

Home Office Officials
1782–1870

compiled by

J. C. SAINTY

UNIVERSITY OF LONDON
INSTITUTE OF HISTORICAL RESEARCH
THE ATHLONE PRESS
1975

Published by
THE ATHLONE PRESS
UNIVERSITY OF LONDON
at 4 Gower Street, London WC1

Distributed by
Tiptree Book Services Ltd
Tiptree, Essex

U.S.A. & Canada
Humanities Press Inc
New Jersey

0 485 17145 7

Printed in Great Britain by
WESTERN PRINTING SERVICES LTD
BRISTOL

Contents

CONTENTS

Abbreviations

app.	appointed, appointment	occ.	occurrence, occurred
Bart.	Baronet	pd.	paid
c.	circa	pt.	part
cr.	created	reapp.	reappointed, reappointment
d.	death, died	Rept.	Report
dis.	dismissed	res.	resigned
ed.	edited, edition	ret.	retired, retirement
f., ff.	folio, folios	succ.	succeeded
HC	House of Commons Paper	TM	Treasury Minute
Hon.	Honourable	vac.	vacated office, vacation of office

References

IN MANUSCRIPT

Public Record Office, London

AO 3/1102–1105	Declared Accounts: Treasury Solicitor.
BT 5	Board of Trade: Minutes.
C 66	Patent Rolls.
CO 324	Colonial Office: General Entry Books.
HO 36	Home Office: Treasury Entry Books.
HO 42	Home Office: Domestic Letters and Papers.
HO 43	Home Office: General Entry Books.
HO 45	Home Office: Registered Papers.
HO 82	Home Office: Accounts and Estimates.
HO 88	Home Office: Fee Books.
PC 2	Privy Council Registers.
Prob. 11	Prerogative Court of Canterbury: Registered Copies of Wills.
PRO 30/8/184	Chatham Papers.
SP 44	Secretaries of State: Domestic Entry Books.
SP 45/35	Secretaries of State: Fee Book.
T 1	Treasury Papers.
T 13	Treasury: Letters to Home Office.
T 29	Treasury Minutes.
T 38/14–20	Treasury: Accounts passed.
T 38/742	Treasury: Special Service Accounts.
T 52	Treasury: King's Warrants.
T 197	Treasury: Arrangement Books.

WORKS IN PRINT

1st Rept. on Fees	*First Report from Commissioners for Enquiring into Fees in Public Offices 1786* (HC 1806, vii).
Gent. Mag.	*Gentleman's Magazine.*
Nelson, *Home Office*	R. R. Nelson, *The Home Office 1782–1801.* Durham, N.C. 1969.
Officials of the Secretaries of State	*Officials of the Secretaries of State 1660–1782,* comp. J. C. Sainty. London 1973.
Royal Kal.	*Royal Kalendar.*
16th Rept. on Finance	*Sixteenth Report of Select Committee on Finance 1797.* Reports of Committees of House of Commons 1797–1803, xii.

Note on Editorial Method

This volume is designed to make available lists of the officials who served in the Home Office between the establishment of the department in 1782 and the year 1870 which witnessed the introduction of the system of open competition for entrants into most departments of the Civil Service. This system was not applied to the Home Office until 1873 but, in the interests of uniformity with the rest of the volumes in the series, the end of the year 1870 has been adhered to as the terminal point for the lists. The material is presented in four parts: an introduction, lists of appointments, periodic lists of officials and an alphabetical list of officials. The purpose of the introduction is to provide a short account of the institutional development of the Home Office during the period in order that the various offices and grades may be related to their general context. The lists of appointments give the dates of appointments to these offices and grades. They are preceded by introductory notes which bring together information concerning such matters as the method of appointment, remuneration and other relevant material. The periodic lists enable the complete establishment to be seen at selected dates.

The alphabetical list is not intended to be a biographical index. Its purpose is confined simply to providing summarised accounts of the offices held by each individual within the Home Office during the period. No information has been included unless it is directly relevant to this purpose. Thus dates of death are included only if the individual in question was in office at his death. Appointments to offices outside the Home Office have been ignored unless they occasioned, or can reasonably be held to have occasioned, the departure of the official from the Home Office. In general the accounts of the careers of the 'political' officials, the Secretary of State and the Parliamentary Under Secretary, have been confined to a simple statement of their periods of service in these offices; information concerning resignations and retirements is provided only in the case of those holding 'permanent' offices. Where an individual held an additional office within the Home Office such as a private secretaryship, which was not directly related to the ordinary course of promotion, the details of his period of service in this additional office have been placed in a separate paragraph. The accounts of the careers of those who were in office at the end of 1870 have not been continued beyond this point.

All references have been concentrated in the alphabetical list. Peers and holders of courtesy titles have been indexed under their titles. In the case of change of name or status, appropriate cross-references have been inserted. Unless otherwise noted, information concerning peers and baronets has been taken from the *Complete Peerage* (ed. G. E. C. 2nd ed. 13 vols. London 1910–59), the *Complete Baronetage* (ed. G. E .C. 5 vols. Exeter 1900–6) and *Burke's Peerage*.

Certain conventions have been adopted for dating appointments. Where possible the date selected is that of formal entry into office where this can be ascertained. Thus appointments of Secretaries of State are dated by reference to the day on which they received the seals of office; those of Under Secretaries and Clerks (until 1822) by reference to the letters written to the Post Office in connection with the privilege of franking. Where there is no indication of the date of appointment of an individual, his period of service is dated by reference to the time during which he received a salary or other remuneration or, failing this information, by reference to the earliest and latest date at which he is found occupying a particular office. All officials are taken to have remained in office until the appointment of their successors unless there is clear evidence to support the selection of an earlier date.

Introduction

The Home Office came into existence in 1782 as a result of the decision to reorganise the business undertaken by the Secretaries of State. Originally there had been two Secretaries of State who had shared domestic business. The conduct of foreign affairs, on the other hand, had been divided between them on a geographical basis, an arrangement that had given rise to the designations 'northern' and 'southern' to describe the departments over which they presided. Colonial business formed part of the area of responsibility of the Southern Secretary until 1768 when it was transferred to a third or Colonial Secretary. In 1782 the office of third Secretary of State was abolished. Foreign business was placed exclusively in the hands of one of the remaining Secretaries of State while domestic and colonial business was entrusted to the other. As a consequence the Secretaries of State came to be known as the Foreign and Home Secretaries and their departments as the Foreign and Home Offices.[1]

In institutional terms the Foreign Office took over the staff which had served in the former Northern Department while the Home Office was composed of that of the former Southern Department, supplemented by two of the officials of the abolished Colonial Office.[2] As constituted in March 1782 the Home Office consisted of a Secretary of State, two Under Secretaries, a Chief Clerk and ten other Clerks, the first four of whom were customarily known as Senior Clerks, two Office or Chamber Keepers and a Housekeeper or Necessary Woman. Of these the Secretary of State and the Under Secretaries received salaries from the crown. The Secretary of State, the Under Secretaries, the Chief Clerk and the Office Keepers were also entitled to fixed fees on instruments passing through the office. The Secretary of State was responsible for paying out of his emoluments the salaries of all the Clerks (except the Chief Clerk), the Office Keepers and the Housekeeper. The Clerks also received fixed annual

[1] For the Home Office generally during this period, see E. Troup, *The Home Office*, 2nd ed. (London 1926); F. Newsam, *The Home Office* (London 1954); R. R. Nelson, *The Home Office, 1782–1801* (Durham, N.C. 1969); A. P. Donajgrodzki, 'New roles for old: the Northcote-Trevelyan Report and the clerks of the Home Office 1822–48', *Studies in the growth of nineteenth-century government*, ed. G. Sutherland (London 1972), 82–109. Appointments of Under Secretaries and Clerks between 1782 and 1822 can be found in the letters sent from the Home Office to the Post Office (HO 43). Periods of service can be established from the quarterly salary lists which are complete from 1795 to 1849 and also from the accounts of the contingent fund which are complete from 1788 with the exception of the years 1810–22 (HO 82). Information in this series can be supplemented by other accounts, in particular those of Home Office fees (HO 88). After 1849, when the staff began to be paid directly by the Paymaster General, no salary lists survive nor does any other source in which appointments were systematically recorded. It is, therefore, not always possible to date appointments precisely during this period. Information concerning establishment matters generally may be found in the exchanges of correspondence between the Home Office and the Treasury (HO 36; T 13), in the Treasury Papers (T 1) and in a number of collections surviving amongst the Home Office Papers (HO 45/9283/1782; HO 45/9483/1782).

[2] For the organisation of these departments, see *Officials of the Secretaries of State*, 1–21. Wilmot and Palman were transferred from the Colonial to the Home Office. In June 1782 Pollock, the former Chief Clerk in the Colonial Office, was appointed to the corresponding position in the Home Office. In 1792 C. Peace, another former Clerk in the Colonial Office, was appointed Librarian.

amounts from the Post Office in compensation for the loss of part of the privilege of franking mail.[3]

The responsibilities of the office were increased in May 1782 as a result of the abolition of the Board of Trade which had previously undertaken certain colonial or plantation business. Part of this business had been the function of reporting on the acts of colonial legislatures which had been undertaken by the Counsel to the Board. This function was now entrusted to a Counsel attached to the Home Office.[4] Other colonial business was undertaken on a temporary basis by Elliott, the former Solicitor and Clerk of Reports and acting Secretary of the Board. In 1783 a separate sub-department of the office was formed, known as the Plantation Department, to assume this responsibility. Three Clerks were assigned to it and it was placed in the charge of Elliott who was originally designated Chief Clerk but who was given the rank of Under Secretary in the following year.[5]

In the years 1785–6 the Home and Foreign Offices were investigated by the Commissioners on Fees. The evidence which the Commissioners took from the officials of the two departments and which is included in their first report,[6] affords a valuable insight into the manner in which they were organised at this period. The recommendations made by the Commissioners were in substance the same for both offices. One of the more significant of these was that one of the Under Secretaries should be 'stationary' or permanent and undertake 'the necessary official business' of his department while the other should be appointed by the Secretary of State for the time being and manage his 'private and confidential business'.[7] This proposed differentiation, which had to a certain extent been foreshadowed by earlier conventions in the two offices, eventually formed the basis of the distinction between the 'Permanent' and 'Parliamentary' Under Secretaries. The Commissioners recommended the discontinuation of the arrangements under which officials had received their remuneration in uncertain amounts from a variety of different sources and their replacement by a system whereby all allowances, fees and perquisites were carried to a common fund out of which fixed salaries were paid. They also urged the adoption of regular arrangements for retiring pensions and the abolition of a number of sinecure offices attached to the offices of the Secretaries of State which had been kept in being in order to provide for officials who were no longer active.[8]

Eight years were to elapse before any action was taken on the recommendations of the Commissioners on Fees. In the meantime a number of changes occurred in the structure of the office. In 1787 Elliott, the Under Secretary for the Plantation Department, died and was not replaced.[9] Two years later the three Clerks in the same department were absorbed into the office and the number of Clerks on the ordinary establishment increased to eleven in consequence.[10] In January 1791 the office of Law Clerk, which had formerly been attached to the offices of the Secretaries of State, was revived while in June of the same year Dundas, on his appointment as Home Secretary,

[3] 1st Rept. on Fees, 5–8.
[4] Officials of the Boards of Trade 1660–1782, comp. J. C. Sainty (London 1974), 36–7; TM 24 Feb. 1783 (T 29/53 p. 164).
[5] HO 36/4 pp. 13–18; TM 14 Nov. 1783 (T 29/54 p. 435); 1st Rept. on Fees, 4, 25–6; HO 43/1 p. 331; Nelson, Home Office, 132–4.
[6] 1st Rept. on Fees, 1–48.   [7] ibid. 10.
[8] ibid. 10–12. For the sinecure offices, see Officials of the Secretaries of State, 21, 43–54.
[9] Nelson, Home Office, 134.
[10] HO 43/2 p. 348. A Supernumerary Clerk was appointed in 1791 (ibid. p. 257).

made salaries available for a Private Secretary and a Précis Writer.[11] In November of the same year the Law Clerk, King, was appointed a third Under Secretary. However, this was only a temporary arrangement, made necessary by Nepean's absence abroad, and lasted only until August 1792 when the resignation of Bernard, the other Under Secretary, reduced the number of these officials to two, at which level it remained for the rest of the period covered by these lists.[12]

In October 1792 a Librarian was appointed while in September 1793 the responsibility of keeping the criminal register of felons at Newgate was assumed by the Home Office and entrusted to Raven, an Extra or Supplementary Clerk, who appears also to have taken charge of the growing general criminal business of the department.[13] In July 1794 the office of third Secretary of State was revived and given responsibility for war, Dundas being transferred from the Home Office to fill it. Shortly before his departure he set on foot a plan for retiring four of the older Clerks. He took two other Clerks with him to the War Office. When the arrangements were finally completed by his successor, Portland, no fewer than seven Clerks had been replaced within the space of a year—a turnover that was unparalleled during the period.[14]

It was not until February 1795 that the three Secretaries of State finally submitted their observations on the report of the Commissioners on Fees.[15] They rejected the recommendation that there should be one 'permanent' Under Secretary on the ground that there might be circumstances in which a Secretary of State would be justified in making a change in the holders of both these offices. They agreed to the proposal that all officials should be paid fixed salaries from a single source although they stipulated that the number of Clerks and the general level of remuneration should be higher than that originally recommended. They accepted the principle of making proper provision for retiring pensions. An order in council was thereupon promulgated to give effect to the proposals of the Commissioners as modified by the Secretaries of State. The establishment of the Home Office was fixed at one Secretary of State at £6000, two Under Secretaries at £1500, a Chief Clerk at £1000, eleven other Clerks with salaries ranging from £80 to £650, a Private Secretary and a Précis Writer, each with a salary of £300 and two Office Keepers and a Housekeeper, each with £100. Shortly afterwards the office of Law Clerk, which had been omitted in error, was included in the establishment with a salary of £300.[16] The salaries were to be paid out of a fund to which all the office fees were to be carried. In the event of the fund falling short, deficiencies were to be met by the civil list.[17]

In 1796 the growing criminal business of the department gave rise to the appointment of a Counsel.[18] In 1800 Raven was dismissed and his duties were divided between two other Supplementary Clerks, Capper and Day. The former was appointed Clerk for Criminal Business while the latter was made Keeper of the Criminal Register.[19] Although these offices continued to increase in importance as the nineteenth century proceeded they remained outside the ordinary establishment.

[11] Nelson, *Home Office*, 59–60. [12] ibid. 34–5. [13] ibid. 60–1.
[14] HO 43/5 pp. 176–8; HO 43/6 p. 27; CO 324/107 p. 182. [15] *16th Rept. on Finance*, 309–11.
[16] Orders in council 27 Feb. and 15 April 1795 (ibid. 311–12).
[17] See also Civil List Act 1810 (50 Geo. III, c 117, s 9). Following the Civil List Act 1816 (56 Geo. III, c 46) estimates of the amount of the deficiency of the fee fund were laid before the House of Commons and the sums required voted annually. It was not until 1837 that the estimates presented and the sums voted were described as being for the Home Office itself.
[18] TM 7 March 1799 (T 29/74 p. 179).
[19] Nelson, *Home Office*, 61; HO 82/3, payments 19 Jan., 24 Feb., 20 May and 11 Aug. 1801.

In 1799 the salaries of the Under Secretaries were increased to £2000 with provision for an increase to £2500 after three years' service.[20] In February 1801 it was laid down that the salary of the Chief Clerk should increase from £1000 to £1250 after five years' service.[21] In the following August the responsibility for colonial matters was removed from the Home Office and entrusted to the Secretary of State for War.[22] As a result the Counsel for Colonial Business passed under the authority of the latter. Otherwise there was no change in the structure of the Home Office where no special arrangements had been made for the conduct of colonial business since the abolition of the Plantation Department in 1789.

In 1803 the increase in the business arising from the correspondence relating to the militia, yeomanry and volunteer corps led to the appointment of two additional Clerks, bringing the total number up to thirteen.[23] In 1809 an arrangement was made for the remuneration of the Clerks to increase in proportion to their length of service. Provision was made for £80, £200, £300 and £400 to be added to their salaries after successive periods of five years' service. This arrangement was extended to three officials who remained outside the ordinary establishment, the Librarian, the Clerk for Criminal Business and the Keeper of the Criminal Register.[24]

In 1813 and 1818 respectively the offices of Counsel for Criminal Business and Law Clerk were abolished on the deaths of their holders.[25] In 1817, in response to criticism made by the House of Commons, the period of service required by Under Secretaries before they became entitled to the addition of £500 was extended from three to seven years.[26]

In 1822 parliamentary pressure for economy led to a comprehensive revision of the establishment.[27] The salaries of the Under Secretaries were fixed at £2000 without any provision for an increase for length of service. The previous arrangement under which a particular salary had been accorded to each Clerk with provision for increases after successive periods of five years' service was discontinued and replaced by a system according to which the Clerks were divided into classes to which salary scales with regular annual increments were attached. The Chief Clerk retained his special position with a scale ranging from £1000 to £1250. The remaining thirteen Clerks were divided into three classes, four Senior or First Class Clerks with salaries ranging from £600 to £800 with provision for the most senior to rise to £900, four Assistant or Second Class Clerks with salaries ranging from £350 to £545 and five Junior or Third Class Clerks with salaries ranging from £150 to £300.[28] It was laid down that Clerks should rise according to seniority to the head of their class but that they should not be promoted to a higher class without an express appointment by the Secretary of State. The offices of Private Secretary and Précis Writer were retained with their

[20] Order in council 23 Jan. 1799 (PC 2/152 pp. 157–8).
[21] Order in council 18 Feb. 1801 (HO 45/9283/1782L).
[22] Nelson, *Home Office*, 135; D. M. Young, *The Colonial Office in the Early 19th Century* (London 1961), 11.
[23] Order in council 12 Oct. 1803 (PC 2/164 p. 143).
[24] Order in council 10 May 1809 (HO 45/9283/1782L); order of Earl of Liverpool 5 July 1809 (ibid.).
[25] HC 554 p. 6 (1822) xviii, 150.
[26] Order in council 24 July 1817 (HO 45/9283/1782L).
[27] Order in council 28 March 1822 (ibid.); HC 554 pp. 1–11 (1822) xviii, 145–55.
[28] The Home Office never adopted a consistent terminology to describe its Clerks. For the sake of clarity the terms Senior, Assistant and Junior Clerks have been used throughout these lists.

salaries unchanged. The Librarian and certain subordinate officials were incorporated into the establishment for the first time.

The order in council left open the position of three officials whom it described as 'Supernumerary Clerks'. These were the Keeper of the Criminal Register, the Clerk for Criminal Business and the latter's assistant. It was provided that these posts should remain outside the ordinary establishment while in the hands of their existing holders but that their future should be reconsidered when vacancies occurred. In the event this arrangement was not strictly adhered to. On the resignation of the Assistant Clerk for Criminal Business in 1827 no regular appointment was made, the work being entrusted to Everest who was not employed directly by the Home Office but who received his remuneration as a Clerk on the Convict Hulk Establishment of which his immediate superior, Capper, was Superintendent in addition to his duties as Clerk for Criminal Business.[29] Increasing work led in 1828 to the appointment of an Assistant Keeper of the Criminal Register but this again was not a regular appointment, its holder being paid out of the contingent fund.[30] It is clear that other Extra or Supplementary Clerks were employed in the criminal business of the department on a more or less permanent basis from about this period but, in the absence of sufficiently detailed records, there is no means of establishing precisely their identity or the limits of their service.[31]

In 1831 the position of the Under Secretaries was regulated. Although the Secretaries of State had rejected in 1795 the recommendations made by the Commissioners on Fees with regard to these offices, the practice in the Home Office had nevertheless conformed closely to their proposals. From 1782 one of the offices had been filled by a succession of individuals without seats in parliament whose tenure, while not permanent in a technical sense, had in fact been unaffected by political changes. In the case of the other office, however, it had been accepted that it was at the disposal of the Secretary of State and its holder had, since 1806, invariably sat in the House of Commons. In 1831 a Treasury minute gave formal recognition to these arrangements. The Under Secretaries were for the first time officially designated 'Permanent' and 'Parliamentary' and accorded distinct salaries, £2000 and £1500 respectively.[32] However, although the position of the Permanent Under Secretary was clearly defined from this point, there were two subsequent instances—those of Gregson (1835) and Le Marchant (1847–8)—in which tenure of the 'Parliamentary' under secretaryship was not associated with membership of either house of parliament.

In 1836 the business relating to aliens which had since 1793 been conducted by a separate department under the authority of the Secretary of State was transferred to the Home Office and entrusted to a former Clerk of that department who was brought onto the strength of the office.[33] In 1837 the status of the office of Parliamentary Counsel to the Home Office was given final definition. This post had had its origin in the arrangements made by Peel as Home Secretary for the reform and consolidation of the criminal law. The task of drafting the necessary measures had been entrusted principally to William Gregson. Gregson, although not in possession of a formal

[29] Order in council 13 Jan. 1845 (HO 45/9283/1782G).
[30] HO 82/3, payment 5 April 1828.   [31] HO 82/18, Home Office Estimates.
[32] *Rept. of Select Committee on Reduction of Salaries 1831* (HC 322 p. 7 (1830–1) iii, 451); TM 15 April 1831 (HC 375 pp. 3–4 (1830–1) vii, 494–5). See also *Rept. of Select Committee on Miscellaneous Expenditure 1848* (HC 543 pt. i, p. 214 (1847–8) xviii, pt. i, 278).
[33] T 13/1 p. 81. For the Aliens Department, see Nelson, *Home Office*, 123–30.

appointment, was employed between 1826 and 1833 on a continuous basis by successive Secretaries of State to prepare parliamentary bills relating both to criminal and other matters.[34] Gregson ceased to act in this capacity in 1833 and was not immediately replaced, the necessary work being undertaken by a number of different draftsmen during the next two years.[35] In 1835 Russell obtained authority for the appointment of a salaried Parliamentary Counsel to be permanently attached to the Home Office.[36] In the following year the Counsel was allowed the services of two Clerks[37] while the office itself was formally included in the establishment in 1837.[38]

In February 1841 it was found necessary to appoint a Solicitor to undertake the legal work of the department but this official resigned in September of the same year and was not replaced.[39] In 1842, as part of the arrangements made by the Treasury for the conduct of the legal business of the government, the work of the Parliamentary Counsel was considerably extended and the holder of the post, while remaining on the establishment of the Home Office, became in effect the principal draftsman to the government. At the same time the duties formerly undertaken by the Home Office Solicitor were transferred to the Treasury Solicitor.[40]

In October 1841 the offices of Keeper and Assistant Keeper of the Criminal Register were finally regulated by order in council.[41] In 1845 similar action was taken with regard to Everest, the Assistant Clerk for Criminal Business, who was then brought officially onto the strength of the Home Office. In 1847 Everest succeeded to the senior position on the retirement of Capper. However, although regulated by order in council, these posts still remained outside the ordinary establishment.[42]

In 1848 the state of the office was such that the Home Secretary, Grey, considered that it should be the subject of a comprehensive enquiry. The Treasury concurred and a committee consisting of Lewis, the Parliamentary Under Secretary, Sir Charles Trevelyan, the Assistant Secretary of the Treasury and W. Gibson Craig, one of the Junior Lords of the Treasury, was appointed for the purpose. Grey accepted the substance of the recommendations contained in their report when preparing his minute of 22 January 1849 outlining his reform of the office.[43] It was evident that the work was very unequally distributed amongst the Clerks. Some of the most senior and highly paid were underemployed while others who were in less favourable positions were overburdened. The organisation had become inflexible partly because of the practice of granting special allowances for particular tasks—a practice which militated against the principle that the whole of an official's time should be at the disposal of the public. Much inconvenience and unnecessary expense had been incurred because the criminal department had been staffed by a separate group of Clerks and kept wholly distinct from the rest of the establishment. Grey authorised a rearrangement of the duties of

---

[34] T 38/16 p. 294; T 29/344 p. 399; J. A. Gulland, 'The history of the criminal law reforms of the period of Peel's home secretaryship, 1822–1827', *Bull. Inst. Hist. Research*, viii (1930–1), 182–5; H. Parris, *Constitutional Bureaucracy* (London 1969), 174–7.

[35] HO 36/23 pp. 323, 328, 333–4, 334–5, 439–50.

[36] HO 36/24 pp. 161–2; T 13/1 pp. 65, 91, 109.

[37] TM 5 May 1836 (T 29/377 pp. 119–20.)

[38] Order in council 1 March 1837 (PC 2/219 p. 190).

[39] HO 36/26 pp. 51, 55–6, 148–9, 402; T 13/1 pp. 297, 320.

[40] TM 18 March 1842 (HC 543, pt. ii pp. 170–2 (1847–8) xviii, pt. ii, 176–8).

[41] Order in council 6 Oct. 1841 (HO 45/9283/1782L).

[42] Orders in council 13 Jan. 1845, 17 June 1847 (HO 45/9283/1782G).

[43] HO 45/9483/1782M1; HO 45/9483/1782M2; HO 36/29 pp. 272–3, 275, 384–93.

the office based on a more rational distribution of work. Henceforth criminal business was to be considered part of the ordinary business of the department to which any Clerk could be assigned.

The principal changes in the establishment were sanctioned by an order in council[44] which authorised a reduction in the salary of the Chief Clerk and provided that for the future the first Senior Clerk should receive the addition of £100 to his salary only when he was in charge of one of the three branches into which the work of the office was divided. The salary of the Clerk for Criminal Business was assimilated to that of a Senior Clerk. The office of Précis Writer was abolished while the duties of the Librarian, who was given the additional title of Registrar, were extended. Grey accepted the recommendations of the committee to the effect that future appointments to the establishment should be subject to previous examination and to one year's probation, and that promotion from grade to grade should be made by selection according to merit and qualification. In implementing these reforms he was assisted by the fact that the Chief Clerk, two Senior Clerks and the Librarian, who also held the office of Précis Writer, all retired early in 1849. In selecting the new Chief Clerk he took the unusual step of promoting H. J. Knyvett over the heads of two Clerks who were more senior to him in point of service. Grey filled two of the vacancies on the establishment by transferring to them two Supplementary or Extra Clerks, Joseph and Maconochie, who had already given proof of their competence in the office. Finally the post of Clerk for Aliens Business was abolished and its former holder appointed to the vacant office of Librarian and Registrar.[45]

In 1851, on the abolition of the Signet Office, the residual functions connected with the Signet were transferred to the Home Office together with one of its former officials who was accorded the title of Clerk for Signet Business.[46] In May 1852 the remuneration of the two Supplementary Clerks attached to the Criminal Branch was revised. Previously they had been paid at a fixed weekly rate. They were now accorded salaries with provision for increases for successive periods of five years.[47] In August of the same year an application was made for an increase in the establishment to deal with the additional work thrown on the office by recent legislation. The Treasury agreed to an addition of one permanent and one supernumerary Junior Clerk.[48] In 1854 the supernumerary was made permanent thus bringing the total number of Junior Clerks up to seven.[49] In 1853 the business connected with turnpike roads and highways was taken over by the Home Office. Three Clerks formerly employed by the Surveyor of Roads were transferred to the department. One was given a special position and salary as Clerk for Roads Business while the other two were classed as Supplementary Clerks.[50]

In 1856 Grey, the Home Secretary, obtained Treasury consent to a further enquiry into the establishment. A committee was appointed consisting of Massey, the Parliamentary Under Secretary, H. B. W. Brand, Grey's former Private Secretary who was now a Junior Lord of the Treasury, and G. Arbuthnot who, as Auditor of the Civil List, was one of the senior permanent officials of the Treasury. Their report was dated 22 July 1856.[51] Despite the recommendation of 1848 the committee found that the

---

[44] Order in council 13 Feb. 1849 (HO 45/9283/1782L).   [45] HO 36/29 pp. 394–6.
[46] T 13/3 p. 287.   [47] HO 36/30 pp. 34, 369; HO 36/32 pp. 374–8.
[48] HO 36/30 pp. 409–10; order in council 18 Aug. 1852 (HO 45/9283/1782L).
[49] HO 36/31 pp. 205–6; order in council 9 March 1854 (PC 2/239 p. 220).
[50] HO 36/31 pp. 34–5; T 13/3 p. 414.
[51] HO 45/9483/1782M5. There is another copy in T 1/6258A/13006.

appointment of new Clerks had not been subject to a preliminary examination or to a period of probationary service. However, they recognised that this state of affairs would be rectified as soon as new entrants began to be examined by the Civil Service Commissioners in conformity with the order in council of the previous year. They found that discipline in the office was defective and recommended that records of attendance should be kept and examined when promotions from one grade to another came to be considered. Apart from the case of the Chief Clerk appointed by Grey in 1849 such promotions had in the past been governed solely by reference to seniority. The committee confirmed the recommendation made by its predecessor in 1848 and urged that 'merit and capacity' should be the main considerations and that seniority should be only one of a number of claims to promotion.

The committee found that the business of the office was divided into three principal branches, known as the Commissions and Patents, the Domestic and the Criminal. They proposed that a fourth, to be known as the Police or Statistical Branch, should be placed under S. Redgrave, the Keeper of the Criminal Register who, together with Everest, the Clerk for Criminal Business, should be considered supernumerary Senior Clerks. As vacancies occurred the opportunity should be taken of reducing the number of Senior Clerks to three who, together with the Chief Clerk, would preside over the four branches. The committee did not feel any further reduction in the number of Clerks to be justified but urged that, as the amount of work increased, the practice of entrusting the more routine tasks to Supplementary Clerks should be extended. The latter should be divided into two classes to conform with arrangements already adopted in other departments. The committee recommended that the establishment should ultimately consist of a Chief Clerk with a fixed salary of £1000, three Senior Clerks, six Assistant Clerks and seven Junior Clerks with scales ranging from £650 to £900, from £350 to £600 and from £100 to £300 respectively, and a Librarian.

The new Statistical Branch was formed as soon as the report was received but otherwise no immediate steps were taken to implement its recommendations.[52] In August 1856 the system of examination by the Civil Service Commissioners was applied for the first time to a candidate for a junior clerkship on the establishment. This arrangement was extended to the Supplementary Clerks in 1859 and to the subordinate staff in 1861.[53] In 1858 the remuneration of Redgrave, the head of the Police and Statistical Branch, was brought into line with that of a Senior Clerk as recommended by the committee of 1856.[54] In February 1860 a similar arrangement was made for Everest, the Clerk in charge of the Criminal Branch.[55] In the following March Redgrave retired and his branch was entrusted to Leslie, one of the Senior Clerks on the ordinary establishment, with a salary of £900. The number of Assistant Clerks was increased from four to five and the class of Junior Clerks reduced from seven to six. It was also provided that the starting salary of newly appointed Junior Clerks should be £100 instead of £150. At the same time the Treasury attempted to secure an undertaking from the Home Office that, in conformity with the recommendation of the committee of 1856, no further appointment to the grade of Senior Clerk

[52] Minute of 29 Aug. 1856 (HO 45/9483/1782M5A).
[53] HO 43/89 p. 53; HO 43/93 p. 288; HO 43/96 p. 404. Although the system of open competition for entrants was introduced into most departments in 1870, it was not adopted by the Home Office until 1873 (M. Wright, *Treasury Control of the Civil Service 1854-1874* (Oxford 1969), 94-6).
[54] HO 36/32 pp. 374-8; T 13/5 pp. 221-2; HO 45/9483/1782M6A.
[55] T 13/5 pp. 340-1; T 1/6258A/13006.

should be made until the number had been reduced to three. This the Secretary of State refused to give and the Treasury marked its displeasure by declining to pursue a proposal for an improvement in the salaries of the Assistant Clerks.[56]

In 1861 the position of the Supplementary Clerks was regulated. As suggested in 1856 they were divided into two classes, the first consisting of four Clerks and the second of three, with salary scales ranging from £150 to £300 and £100 to £150 respectively.[57] In August 1865 the office of Librarian and Registrar was abolished and its duties distributed amongst the Clerks on the establishment. At the same time the number of Assistant Clerks was increased from five to six.[58] In the following October the retirement of H. J. Knyvett, the Chief Clerk, became effective. He was replaced by C. R. Fitzgerald who was, with Treasury approval, at once accorded a salary of £1000, the maximum on the scale authorised in 1849.[59] J. Streatfield, one of the Senior Clerks on the old establishment, was placed in charge of the vacant branch with an increased salary of £900. The place of the fourth Senior Clerk was filled by the promotion of an Assistant Clerk, Dillon, who was not given any particular responsibility. Reverting to the stand which it had taken in 1860 the Treasury objected strongly to the last appointment, pointing out that it was in conflict with the recommendation of the committee of 1856 according to which each Senior Clerk should superintend a branch of business. Eventually agreement was reached that no further Senior Clerks should be appointed until the number had been reduced to three, including the Clerk for Criminal Business, and that, as vacancies occurred, they should be filled by the recruitment of additional Junior Clerks. At the same time the Treasury authorised improved salary arrangements granting the Chief Clerk a scale ranging from £1000 to £1200, the three Senior Clerks in charge of branches of business a scale ranging from £700 to £1000 and the Assistant Clerks a scale ranging from £350 to £600. Finally it was provided that, as soon as the existing anomalies had been removed, the establishment should be fixed at one Chief, three Senior, seven Assistant and eight Junior Clerks.[60]

In February 1866 the financial position of Sanders, the Clerk for Signet Business, was regulated and improved.[61] In the following June the salaries of the Supplementary Clerks were increased and the appointment of a fourth Second Class Supplementary Clerk authorised.[62] In December two Clerks, who had previously been employed on a temporary basis to prepare local taxation returns, were given permanent standing in the office.[63]

In December 1867 Anderson, a barrister previously employed by the Irish government, was brought to London and attached to the Home Office to give advice on the problems caused by the Fenian conspiracy. His appointment was originally intended to be purely temporary but it was found necessary to retain his services indefinitely as Assistant on Irish Affairs.[64] In February 1868 one Assistant and one Junior Clerk were added to the establishment, to deal with the increasing work, bringing the numbers in these grades to eight and six respectively.[65] In March the Treasury

[56] T 13/5 pp. 348-9, 358-9, 367-9; T 1/6258A/13006. [57] T 1/6309A/11602.
[58] HO 36/34 p. 482; T 1/1599B/18996. [59] HO 36/35 pp. 37-9; T 13/7 p. 28; T 1/6599B/18996.
[60] HO 36/35 pp. 93, 159; T 13/7 pp. 126-8; T 1/6599B/18996; T 1/6661B/19489.
[61] HO 36/35 pp. 166, 192; T 1/6661B/19489.
[62] T 13/7 pp. 209-10; T 1/6599B/18996; T 1/6661B/19489.
[63] HO 36/35 pp. 296, 334-5, 357-8; T 13/7 pp. 273-4, 319; T 1/6661B/19489.
[64] HO 36/36 pp. 249-50, 291, 432, 483; T 13/8 pp. 45-6, 169, 188; T 1/6943A/21356.
[65] HO 36/36 pp. 179-80; T 13/7 pp. 541-2.

authorised the appointment of an Accountant to supervise the preparation of the accounts of the various agencies for which the Secretary of State was responsible.[66] In accordance with the arrangement made in 1866 the vacancies which occurred amongst the Senior Clerks in November 1868 and February 1869 were filled by the appointment of two additional Junior Clerks.[67] In February 1869 a new arrangement was made for the drafting of government bills which involved the transfer of the office of Parliamentary Counsel from the Home Office to the Treasury.[68] The Home Office thereby lost the assistance of an official upon whom it had come to rely for advice on a wide range of topics not immediately connected with the drafting of bills. To make good this deficiency the office of Legal Adviser was created in October of the same year.[69]

In 1870 the Home Secretary, Bruce, appointed a departmental committee, consisting of Rutson, his Private Secretary, Knatchbull Hugessen, the Parliamentary Under Secretary, and the Earl of Morley, a Lord in Waiting and the departmental representative in the House of Lords, to investigate the establishment. Their comprehensive report,[70] dated 9 December, contains a large amount of information about the staff and organisation of the office. The committee made a number of recommendations which were discussed with the Treasury. The consequential changes were not implemented until the following year and are, therefore, outside the scope of this volume.

[66] HO 36/36 pp. 221, 226; T 13/8 p. 15.
[68] T 13/8 pp. 185, 188.
[70] HO 45/9283/1782MA.

[67] HO 43/114 pp. 165, 452.
[69] ibid. pp. 381, 386; T 1/6943A/21356.

Secretary of State 1782–1870

The Secretary of State entered office on receiving the seals from the Sovereign. He took the oath at a meeting of the Privy Council, usually held on the same day.[1] His authority lasted until he delivered the seals back to the Sovereign. Originally appointments were formally embodied in letters patent under the great seal granting the office during pleasure. This practice was abandoned after the appointment of Grey in 1861.[2]

From 1782 to 1795 the Secretary of State received fixed allowances amounting to £5680 a year together with office fees and other minor perquisites, the total of which varied from year to year.[3] In 1795 a consolidated salary of £6000 was substituted.[4] In 1831 this was reduced to £5000.[5]

LIST OF APPOINTMENTS

1782	27 March	Shelburne, Earl of	1830	22 Nov.	Melbourne, Viscount
1782	10 July	Townshend, T.	1834	19 July	Duncannon, Viscount
1783	2 April	North, Lord	1834	17 Nov.	Wellington, Duke of[7]
1783	19 Dec.	Temple, Earl[6]	1834	15 Dec.	Goulburn, H.
1783	23 Dec.	Sydney, Lord	1835	18 April	Russell, Lord J.
1789	5 June	Grenville, W. W.	1839	2 Sept.	Normanby, Marquess of
1791	8 June	Dundas, H.			
1794	11 July	Portland, Duke of	1841	3 Sept.	Graham, Sir J. R. G.
1801	30 July	Pelham, Lord	1846	6 July	Grey, Sir G.
1803	17 Aug.	Yorke, C. P.	1852	27 Feb.	Walpole, S. H.
1804	11 May	Hawkesbury, Lord	1852	28 Dec.	Palmerston, Viscount
1806	5 Feb.	Spencer, Earl	1855	8 Feb.	Grey, Sir G.
1807	25 March	Hawkesbury, Lord	1858	26 Feb.	Walpole, S. H.
1809	1 Nov.	Ryder, Hon. R.	1859	3 March	Sotheron Estcourt, T. H. S.
1812	11 June	Sidmouth, Viscount			
1822	17 Jan.	Peel, R.	1859	18 June	Lewis, Sir G. C.
1827	30 April	Sturges Bourne, W.	1861	25 July	Grey, Sir G.
1827	16 July	Lansdowne, Marquess of	1866	6 July	Walpole, S. H.
			1867	17 May	Hardy, G.
1828	22 Jan.	Peel, R.	1868	9 Dec.	Bruce, H. A.

[1] However, Peel did not take the oath until 26 Jan. 1828 although app. on 22 Jan. In the cases of Hawkesbury (1804), Normanby (1839) and Grey (1855) where the Home Secretary was transferred directly from another department of state, no fresh oath was taken.
[2] HO 45/O.S. 8745/1; HO 45/O.S. 8745/1A; HO 45/O.S. 8745/2.
[3] *1st Rept. on Fees*, 5–6, 10, 38–9; Nelson, *Home Office*, 23–4.
[4] Order in council 27 Feb. 1795 (*16th Rept. on Finance*, 311).
[5] TM 15 April 1831 (HC 375 p. 2 (1830–1) vii, 494).
[6] Temporarily held the seals of the Home and Foreign Departments.
[7] Temporarily held the seals of the Home, Foreign and Colonial Departments.

Under Secretaries 1782–1870

In 1782 the Home Office adopted the convention, which had long operated in the Southern Department, of having two Under Secretaries.[1] With the exception of the years 1791–2 when the number rose temporarily to three, this convention was observed until the end of the period.[2] The modern distinction between the Permanent and Parliamentary Under Secretary evolved only gradually and was not the result of any specific decision. The Commissioners on Fees recommended in 1786 that it should be an established rule that one of the Under Secretaries should have security of tenure or be 'stationary'.[3] However, this concept was rejected by the Secretaries of State in their report of 1795 on the ground that it placed undue restriction on their freedom of action. The order in council of that year which settled the establishment of the office made provision for two undifferentiated Under Secretaries.[4] It was not until 1831 that the designations 'Permanent' and 'Parliamentary' were first officially applied to the occupants of these posts.[5]

Nevertheless, although its status remained undefined until 1831, the position of 'permanent' Under Secretary is already discernible at the time of the creation of the Home Office in 1782. Bell had originally been appointed to the Southern Department in 1781 on the understanding that he would succeed to 'what is considered the fix'd and Resident' Under Secretary.[6] The latter position was then held by Sir Stanier Porten who retired in March 1782. Bell was succeeded in his turn by Nepean. During Nepean's absence between 1791 and 1792 his place was taken by an additional Under Secretary, King, who remained in office as a full Under Secretary following the resignation of Bernard, the 'non-permanent' Under Secretary, in the latter year. There were thus two 'permanent' Under Secretaries between 1792 and 1794 when, on Nepean's departure from the Home Office, King became the sole such Under Secretary. King was succeeded in turn by Beckett, Hobhouse and Phillipps, the last of whom was the first to be officially designated Permanent Under Secretary.[7]

The other Under Secretary was customarily 'non-permanent' in the sense that he tended to leave office with the Secretary of State who had appointed him or, later, when the administration to which he owed political allegiance resigned. However, although the office had a marked personal or political character compared with its

[1] *Officials of the Secretaries of State*, 26–7; Nelson, *Home Office*, 26–45.

[2] This leaves out of account Elliott, Under Secretary for the Plantation Department 1784–7. See p. 22.

[3] *1st Rept. on Fees*, 10.

[4] Order in council 27 Feb. 1795 (*16th Rept. on Finance*, 309–11).

[5] TM 15 April 1831 (HC 375 p. 2 (1830–1) vii, 494). In the following lists appointments have been grouped into separate lines of succession from 1782 in order to illustrate the evolution of the two offices. In the alphabetical lists of officials the terms 'Permanent' and 'Parliamentary' have been applied to Under Secretaries only from 1831. See also D. J. Heasman, 'The Emergence and Evolution of the Office of Parliamentary Secretary', *Parliamentary Affairs*, xxiii (1969–70), 345–65.

[6] Nelson, *Home Office*, 28.

[7] For the position of Phillipps, see 'Extracts from Lord Hatherton's Diary', ed. A. Aspinall, *Parliamentary Affairs*, xvii (1964), 377.

counterpart, it was not at first necessarily 'parliamentary' in nature. The post was held by a succession of M.P.s from 1782 to 1794 but between the latter date and 1806 no Under Secretary had a seat in the House of Commons with the exceptions of Greville (1795–6) and Pole Carew (1803–4). After 1806 there was a general expectation that the holders of the office would be members of one or other House. Nevertheless, even after the position was regulated in 1831, there were two cases, those of Gregson (1835) and Le Marchant (1847–8), in which the 'Parliamentary' Under Secretary had no seat in Parliament.[8]

Until 1831 both Under Secretaries received the same remuneration. From 1782 to 1795 this consisted of a salary of £500 from the civil list together with office fees and other small allowances.[9] While King acted as additional Under Secretary between December 1791 and August 1792 his remuneration was limited to £600 a year paid out of the contingent fund.[10] In 1795 the salary of each Under Secretary was fixed at £1500.[11] In 1799 this was raised to £2000 with provision for an increase to £2500 after three years' service.[12] In 1817 the period of service required to qualify for the increase was extended to seven years for future occupants of the offices.[13] In 1822 the salary was reduced to £2000 without any increase for length of service.[14] In 1831 a distinction was made between the remuneration of the Permanent and Parliamentary Under Secretary. The salary of the former was fixed at £2000; that of the latter at £1500.[15]

LISTS OF APPOINTMENTS

PERMANENT UNDER SECRETARY

1782	27 March	Bell, J.		1827	31 July	Phillipps, S. M.
1782	April	Nepean, E.[16]		1848	15 May	Waddington, H.
1791	3 Dec.	King, J.[17]		1867	14 Aug.	Liddell,
1806	18 Feb.	Beckett, J.				Hon. A. F. O.
1817	28 June	Hobhouse, H.				

NON-PERMANENT (LATER PARLIAMENTARY) UNDER SECRETARY

1782	1 April	Nepean, E. [18]		1784	20 Feb.	Townshend,
1782	April	Orde, T.				Hon. J. T.
1782	15 July	Strachey, H.		1789	6 June	Bernard, S.
1783	April	North, Hon. G. A.		1794	17 July	Brodrick, Hon. T.

[8] In 1848 Le Marchant described the office which he held as 'the Parliamentary Secretary, the removable secretary' (*Rept. of Select Committee on Miscellaneous Expenditure 1848* (HC 543, pt. i p. 214 (1847–8) xviii, pt. 1, 278)).

[9] *1st Rept. on Fees*, 19; Nelson, *Home Office*, 40–3.

[10] HO 82/3, payment 12 Nov. 1792. King also received a salary of £300 as Law Clerk.

[11] Order in council 27 Feb. 1795 (*16th Rept. on Finance*, 311).

[12] Order in council 23 Jan. 1799 (PC 2/152 pp. 157–8).

[13] Order in council 24 July 1817 (HO 45/9283/1782L).

[14] Order in council 28 March 1822 (ibid.).

[15] TM 15 April 1831 (HC 375 p. 2 (1830–1) vii, 494).

[16] Became 'permanent' Under Secretary on Bell's resignation.

[17] Additional Under Secretary 3 Dec. 1791–23 Aug. 1792; associate 'permanent' Under Secretary with Nepean 3 Dec. 1791–11 July 1794.

[18] Not an M.P. while Under Secretary.

1796	14 March	Greville, C.	1841	3 Sept.	Manners Sutton, Hon. J. H. T.
1798	1 March	Wickham, W.[19]			
1801	19 Feb.	Finch Hatton, E.[19]	1846	July	Somerville, Sir W. M.
1801	18 Aug.	Shee, Sir G.[19]	1847	22 July	Le Marchant, Sir D.[19]
1803	17 Aug.	Pole Carew, R.	1848	15 May	Lewis, G. C.
1804	27 July	Smyth, J. H.[19]	1850	July	Pleydell Bouverie, Hon. E.
1806	5 Feb.	Williams Wynn, C. W.	1852	Feb.	Jolliffe, Sir W. G. H.
1807	30 Nov.	Jenkinson, Hon. C. C. C.	1852	Dec.	Fitzroy, Hon. H.
			1855	March	Cowper, Hon. W. F.
1810	27 Feb.	Goulburn, H.	1855	Aug.	Massey, W. N.
1812	20 Aug.	Addington, J. H.	1858	March	Hardy, G.
1818	22 April	Clive, H.	1859	June	Clive, G.
1822	18 Jan.	Dawson, G. R.	1862	Nov.	Bruce, H. A.
1827	30 April	Perceval, S.	1864	April	Baring, T. G.
1827	16 July	Spring Rice, T.	1866	May	Knatchbull Hugessen, E. H.
1828	22 Jan.	Peel, W. Y.			
1830	5 Aug.	Clerk, Sir G.	1866	7 July	Belmore, Earl of[20]
1830	22 Nov.	Lamb, Hon. G.	1867	Aug.	Fergusson, Sir J.
1834	13 Jan.	Howick, Viscount	1868	Aug.	Hicks Beach, Sir M. E.
1834	23 July	Stanley, E. J.			
1835	3 Jan.	Gregson, W.[19]	1868	Dec.	Knatchbull Hugessen, E. H.
1835	18 April	Maule, Hon. F.			
1841	15 June	Seymour, Lord			

[19] Not an M.P. while Under Secretary.

[20] Member of the House of Lords.

Chief Clerk 1782–1870

The office of Chief, or First, Clerk, which had been a feature of the Southern Department, formed part of the establishment of the Home Office throughout the period. Originally the Chief Clerk, unlike the other Clerks on the establishment, received no salary from the Secretary of State. His remuneration was derived from a fixed proportion of the office fees, £25 from the Irish concordatum fund, two separate sums of £100 from Post Office funds and a variety of other perquisites and allowances.[1] In 1795 a fixed salary of £1000 was substituted.[2] In 1801 provision was made for an increase to £1250 after five years' service.[3] In 1822 the scale was fixed at £1000 rising by annual increments of £50 to £1250.[4] In 1849 this was reduced to £800 rising by annual increments of £25 to £1000.[5] In 1866 it was increased to £1000 rising by annual increments of £50 to £1200.[6]

LIST OF APPOINTMENTS

1782	27 March	Shadwell, R.	1849	5 April	Knyvett, H. J.
1782	1 June	Pollock, W.	1865	1 Oct.	Fitzgerald, C. R.
1816	15 Feb.	Plasket, T. H.	1868	1 Nov.	Leslie, F. S.

[1] *1st Rept. on Fees*, 20; HO 82/1; Nelson, *Home Office*, 54–5.
[2] Order in council 27 Feb. 1795 (*16th Rept. on Finance*, 311).
[3] Order in council 18 Feb. 1801 (HO 45/9283/1782L).
[4] Order in council 28 March 1822 (ibid.).
[5] Order in council 13 Feb. 1849 (ibid.). C. R. Fitzgerald was granted a salary of £1000 immediately on his appointment in 1865 (T 13/7 p. 28).
[6] ibid. pp. 126–8; HO 36/35 p. 159.

Clerks 1782–1822

On its formation in 1782 the Home Office contained, apart from the Chief Clerk, ten established Clerks.[1] The number was increased to eleven in 1789[2] and to thirteen in 1803.[3] A Supernumerary Clerk held office between 1791 and 1794.[4] Between 1782 and 1822 it was the practice for a varying number of the more senior Clerks to be designated 'Senior Clerks' in the published lists of the office.[5] However, the significance of this term, which is only rarely found in the departmental records and is not reflected in any special salary arrangements, is obscure. The number of Clerks so designated was four between 1783 and 1794, three between 1795 and 1803, two between 1804 and 1807, three between 1808 and 1810, two between 1811 and 1815 and four between 1816 and 1822.[6] In 1822 the Clerks were divided into three classes of Senior, Assistant and Junior.

Between 1782 and 1795 the Clerks received their remuneration in the form of salaries from the Secretary of State, allowances from the Post Office and various perquisites.[7] In the latter year they were provided with consolidated salaries from the fee fund, receiving in order of seniority £650, £450, £300, £200, £160, £140, £130, £120, £110, £100 and £80.[8] The two Clerks added to the establishment in 1803 were each accorded salaries of £80.[9] In 1809 provision was made for the salary of each Clerk to be increased according to length of service, the amounts being £80 after five years, £200 after ten years, £300 after fifteen years and £400 after twenty years.[10]

LIST OF APPOINTMENTS

1782	27 March	Brietzcke, C.	1782	27 March	Colleton, J. N.
1782	27 March	Morin, J.	1782	27 March	Chetwynd, Hon. R.
1782	27 March	Randall, G.	1782	27 March	Palman, G. L.
1782	27 March	Higden, W. H.	1783	25 Feb.	Mathias, G. A. V.
1782	27 March	Carrington, G. W.	1784	7 July	Chapman, J.
1782	27 March	Daw, T.	1786	6 Sept.	Hepburn, R.
1782	27 March	Wilmot, E.	1789	9 Jan.	Bradbury, J.

[1] HO 43/1 pp. 12–13.   [2] HO 43/2 p. 348.
[3] Order in council 12 Oct. 1803 (PC 2/164 p. 143).   [4] HO 43/3 p. 257; HO 43/6 p. 27.
[5] *Royal Kal.* (1783–1822). The term is also employed in the *1st Rept. on Fees*, 4, 14, 21–2.
[6] The following are described as Senior Clerks in the published lists between 1783 and 1822: C. Brietzcke (1783–94), Morin (1783), Randall (1783–98), Higden (1783–1805), Carrington (1784–94), Bradbury (Norton) (1795–7), Plasket (1799–1816), R. Douglas (1799–1803), Adams (1806–9), Hicks (1808–22), G. P. Brietzcke (1816–17), R. R. Wood (1816–22), Noble (1817–22), Mills (1820), Medley (1822).
[7] For details of the remuneration of the Clerks during this period, see *1st Rept. on Fees*, 6–7, 21–4; HO 82/1; Nelson, *Home Office*, 51–2, 175.
[8] Order in council 27 Feb. 1795 (*16th Rept. on Finance*, 311).
[9] Order in council 12 Oct. 1803 (PC 2/164 p. 143).
[10] Order in council 10 May 1809 (HO 45/9283/1782L).

1789	9 Jan.	Jessep, J.	1801	10 July	Norris, J. F.
1789	9 Jan.	Chapman, R.	1803	17 Aug.	Venables, T.
1789	22 Aug.	Goddard, C.	1803	19 Oct.	Edgcumbe, F.
1791	17 May	Douglas, R.	1803	19 Oct.	Reynolds, J.
1791	17 May	Gordon, A.	1805	5 July	Jenkinson, R. H.
1794	24 Oct.	Plasket, T. H.	1805	31 Dec.	Willimot, R.
1794	24 Oct.	Adams, W. D.[11]	1810	10 Oct.	Montagu, W.
1794	24 Oct.	Johnston, W. F.	1811	29 June	Walpole, F.
1794	24 Oct.	Hicks, J.	1815	2 Feb.	Whish, H. F.
1794	24 Oct.	Brietzcke, G. P.	1816	15 Feb.	Hoskins, G.
1794	24 Oct.	Lefroy, G. T.	1817	17 Feb.	Douglas, J. D.
1794	24 Oct.	Wood, E.	1817	14 Aug.	Currie, F. J. G.
1795	22 May	Wood, R. R.	1819	5 April	Le Mesurier, T.
1797	7 Aug.	Noble, R. H.	1819	5 July	Dawson, R. S.
1798	6 Feb.	Mills, F. R.	1820	2 May	Knyvett, H. J.
1799	22 Jan.	Medley, R.			

[11] App. Supernumerary Clerk 17 May 1791.

Senior Clerks 1822–70

Although the term 'Senior Clerk' had been used earlier in the Home Office to describe a varying number of the Clerks on the establishment, it was not until 1822 that it was applied to a distinct grade.[1] In that year provision was made for four Senior, or First Class, Clerks. The most senior of these was accorded a salary of £700 rising by annual increments of £20 to £900 while the salaries of the other three were fixed at £600 rising by annual increments of £20 to £800.[2] In 1849 it was provided that the higher salary should be paid to the Clerk in question only if he was at the head of one of the branches into which the work of the department was divided. At the same time the salary of the Clerk for Criminal Business was assimilated to that of a Senior Clerk.[3]

The committee of 1856 recommended that both the Clerk for Criminal Business and the Keeper of the Criminal Register should be ranked as Senior Clerks and that no further appointment should be made to the grade until its numbers had been reduced to three who, together with the Chief Clerk, were to preside over the four branches into which the business was to be divided, and to receive maximum salaries of £900.[4] The salaries of the Keeper of the Criminal Register and the Clerk for Criminal Business were accordingly revised in 1858 and 1860 respectively.[5] On the retirement of the Keeper of the Criminal Register his duties were entrusted to a Senior Clerk on the ordinary establishment.[6] In 1865 the Home Office filled the vacancy which occurred amongst the Senior Clerks although the individual in question had no branch to superintend—an action which was in conflict with the recommendation of the committee of 1856. In 1866, however, the Treasury secured an undertaking that no further appointments would be made until the number of Senior Clerks had been reduced to three, including the Clerk for Criminal Business. At the same time the salaries of the Clerks in charge of branches of business were fixed at £700 rising by annual increments of £25 to £1000.[7] In conformity with the arrangement made in 1866 the senior clerkships which became vacant in 1868 and 1869 remained unfilled, the number of Senior Clerks on the ordinary establishment being thus reduced by two.

[1] See p. 16.
[2] Order in council 28 March 1822 (HO 45/9283/1782L).
[3] Order in council 13 Feb. 1849 (ibid.).
[4] HO 45/9483/1782M5.
[5] HO 36/32 pp. 374–5; T 13/5 pp. 221–2; HO 45/9483/1782M6A; T 13/5 pp. 340–1; T 1/6258A/13006.
[6] T 13/5 pp. 348–9, 358–9, 367–9; T 1/6258A/13006.
[7] HO 36/35 pp. 93, 159; T 13/7 pp. 126–8; T 1/6599B/18996; T 1/6661B/19489.

LIST OF APPOINTMENTS

1822	28 March	Hicks, J.		1841	29 Aug.	Dawson, R. S.
1822	28 March	Wood, R. R.		1849	5 Jan.	Knyvett, H. J.
1822	28 March	Noble, R. H.		1849	19 Feb.	Fitzgerald, C. R.
1822	28 March	Medley, R.		1849	5 April	Leslie, F. S.
1823	24 March	Norris, J. F.		1850	Aug.	Streatfield, J.
1834	29 July	Venables, T.		1852	Nov.	Erskine, C.
1835	23 May	Walpole, F.		1865	1 Oct.	Dillon, Hon. A. E. D.
1837	25 June	Currie, F. J. G.				

Assistant Clerks 1822–70

The grade of Assistant, or Second Class, Clerk was created in 1822 when provision was made for four such Clerks.[1] The number was increased to five in 1860,[2] to six in 1865,[3] to seven in 1866[4] and to eight in 1868.[5] The salary scale attached to the grade in 1822 was £350 rising by annual increments of £15 to £545.[6] In 1866 it was fixed at £350 rising by annual increments of £20 to £600.[7]

LIST OF APPOINTMENTS

1822	28 March	Norris, J. F.	1849	19 Feb.	Redgrave, S.
1822	28 March	Venables, T.	1849	5 April	Dillon, Hon. A. E. D.
1822	28 March	Walpole, F.	1850	Aug.	Maling, H.
1822	28 March	Whish, H. F.	1852	Nov.	Gilly, F. D.
1823	24 March	Hoskins, G.	1854	Feb.	Joseph, A. G.
1827	23 Feb.	Currie, F. J. G.	1860	March	Maconochie, A.
1828	10 July	Dawson, R. S.	1860	March	Arbuthnot, R. C.
1834	29 July	Knyvett, H. J.	1865	June	Knyvett, C. J.
1835	23 May	Fitzgerald, C. R.	1865	Oct.	Hobhouse, E. A. S.
1837	25 June	Leslie, F. S.	1866	Jan.	Murdoch, C. S.
1841	29 Aug.	Streatfield, J.	1868	Feb.	Campbell, C. G.
1849	5 Jan.	Erskine, C.			

[1] Order in council 28 March 1822 (HO 45/9283/1782L).
[2] T 13/5 pp. 348–9.
[3] HO 36/34 p. 482; T 1/1599B/18996.
[4] T 13/7 pp. 126–8.
[5] HO 36/36 pp. 179–80; T 13/7 pp. 541–2.
[6] Order in council 28 March 1822 (HO 45/9283/1782L).
[7] T 13/7 pp. 126–8.

Junior Clerks 1822–70

The grade of Junior, or Third Class, Clerk was created in 1822 when provision was made for five such Clerks.[1] The number was increased to six in 1852, the appointment of a supernumerary Junior Clerk being authorised at the same time.[2] It was fixed at seven in 1854 when the supernumerary appointment was made permanent.[3] It was reduced to six in 1860 and to five in 1866. In the latter year it was provided that, as vacancies occurred in two of the senior clerkships, they should be filled by the appointment of additional Junior Clerks.[4] In February 1868 the appointment of a sixth Junior Clerk was authorised.[5] In November 1868 and March 1869 seventh and eighth Junior Clerks were appointed to fill the vacancies caused by the abolition of the senior clerkships.[6] The salary scale attached to the grade in 1822 was £150 rising by annual increments of £10 to £300.[7] In 1860 it was provided that, in the case of future appointments, the starting level should be £100.[8]

LIST OF APPOINTMENTS

1822	28 March	Hoskins, G.	1849	19 Feb.	Maconochie, A.
1822	28 March	Currie, F. J. G.	1849	April	Arbuthnot, R. C.
1822	28 March	Le Mesurier, T.	1850	Aug.	Noyes, T. H.
1822	28 March	Dawson, R. S.	1852	9 Aug.	Knyvett, C. J.
1822	28 March	Knyvett, H. J.	1852	9 Aug.	O'Grady, Hon. P. S.
1823	30 March	Fitzgerald, C. R.	1852	Nov.	Perceval, J. S.
1826	8 June	Streatfield, E.	1854	Dec.	Hobhouse, E. A. S.
1827	31 March	Leslie, F. S.	1856	5 Aug.	Murdoch, C. S.
1828	5 April	Streatfield, J.	1856	1 Sept.	Campbell, C. G.
1829	5 Jan.	Anstruther, R.	1860	20 April	Wharton, R.
1834	29 July	Erskine, C.	1861	9 Feb.	Stapleton, E. J.
1835	23 May	Lister, C.	1865	9 Aug.	McClintock, F. R.
1837	25 June	Smith, W.	1865	20 Nov.	Defell, C.
1839	5 April	Redgrave, S.	1868	24 Feb.	Mitford, R. S.
1840	10 Feb.	Dillon, Hon. A. E. D.	1868	24 Feb.	Orr, J. S.
1841	30 Aug.	Maling, H.	1868	26 Nov.	Fitzgerald, G. B.
1847	30 Aug.	Gilly, F. D.	1869	19 March	Dunbar, W. C.
1849	5 Jan.	Joseph, A. G.	1870	4 Feb.	Graves, A. P.

[1] Order in council 28 March 1822 (HO 45/9283/1782L).
[2] Order in council 18 Aug. 1852 (ibid.).
[3] Order in council 9 March 1854 (PC 2/239 p. 220).
[4] T 13/5 pp. 348–9; T 13/7 pp. 126–8.
[5] HO 36/36 pp. 178–9; T 13/7 pp. 541–2.
[6] HO 43/114 pp. 165, 452.
[7] Order in council 28 March 1822 (HO 45/9283/1782L).
[8] T 13/5 pp. 348–9.

Chief Clerk and Under Secretary
(Plantation Department) 1783–7

This office was created in 1783 when Elliott, the former Solicitor and Clerk of Reports of the old Board of Trade, was placed in charge of the department with the title of Chief Clerk and a salary of £500. In the following year he was advanced to the rank of Under Secretary. The office was not filled after Elliott's death in 1787.[1]

APPOINTMENT

1783   Dec.   Elliott, G.

Clerks (Plantation Department) 1783–9

The number of Clerks in the Plantation Department was fixed at three in 1783 with salaries of £120, £100 and £80. The offices ceased to exist in 1789 when the then Clerks were transferred to the ordinary establishment.[2]

LIST OF APPOINTMENTS

| 1783 | Dec. | Bradbury, J. | 1783 | Dec. | Jessep, J. |
| 1783 | Dec. | Porter, J. | 1786 | Aug. | Chapman, R. |

[1] HO 36/4 pp. 13–18; *1st Rept. on Fees*, 25–6; HO 43/1 p. 331; Nelson, *Home Office*, 132–4.
[2] HO 36/4 pp. 13–18; *1st Rept. on Fees*, 26; HO 43/2 p. 348; Nelson, *Home Office*, 133.

Supplementary Clerks 1793–1870

It was the practice of the Home Office from the time of its formation to employ a varying number of Clerks in addition to those on the establishment.[1] However, it was apparently only from 1793 that they were paid out of the funds of the department.[2] The designation of these Clerks varied considerably. At first known usually as Extra or Assistant Clerks they had come by the middle of the nineteenth century to be described as Supplementary Clerks, a term that has, for the sake of consistency, been used throughout these lists. In the cases of the Keeper and Assistant Keeper of the Criminal Register and the Clerk and Assistant Clerk of Criminal Business the practice of employing Supplementary Clerks gave rise to the creation of distinct posts within the structure of the department.

Some Supplementary Clerks, often hired from law stationers, were employed on a purely temporary basis. Others succeeded in acquiring a more or less permanent standing in the office. Two such Clerks were employed in the criminal branch although their identity and limits of service cannot be established with precision before 1859.[3] In 1853 two Supplementary Clerks were transferred to the Home Office in connection with the business arising from highways and turnpike trusts.[4] In 1859 the Supplementary Clerks numbered seven.[5] Originally the usual rate of pay had been five shillings a day (£78 a year). In 1852 salary arrangements similar to those for Supplementary Clerks in the Treasury were introduced which ranged from £109 10s for less than five years' service, to £182 10s for more than twenty years' service.[6] In 1861 the Supplementary Clerks were divided into two classes, the first consisting of four with a salary scale beginning at £150 and rising by annual increments of £10 to £300 and the second consisting of three beginning at £100 and rising by annual increments of £5 to £150.[7] In 1866 new scales were authorised. The salaries of the first class were fixed at £250 rising by annual increments of £10 to £350 while those of the second, now increased to four Clerks, were fixed at £100 rising by annual increments of £5 to £250.[8]

LIST OF APPOINTMENTS

1793	3 Feb.	Raven, E.	1818	5 May	Redgrave, S.
1794	20 April	Capper, J. H.	1839	1 July	Joseph, A. G.
1798	25 March	Peace, W.	1845	8 May	Rowe, G.
1808	21 March	Gaitskell, H.	1845	6 Oct.	Dowling, R. H.
1808		Trushard, P.	1846	Aug.	Playford, H.

[1] *1st Rept. on Fees*, 21; *Rept. of Select Committee on Miscellaneous Expenditure 1848* (HC 543, pt. i p. 214 (1847–8) xviii, pt. i, 278).
[2] *16th Rept. on Finance*, 325.
[3] HO 36/29 pp. 272–3; HO 82/18.
[4] HO 36/31 pp. 34–5; T 13/3 p. 414.
[5] T 1/6309A/11602.
[6] HO 36/30 pp. 34, 369; HO 36/32 pp. 374–8.
[7] T 1/6309A/11602.
[8] T 13/7 pp. 209–10; T 1/6599B/18996; T 1/6661B/19489.

1848	12 March	Maconochie, A.	1856	9 July	Bentham, M. G.
1853	8 April	Paradise, J.	1859	10 Aug.	Mills, F.
1853	8 April	Headland, W. J.	1864	24 Dec.	Cranston, R.
1853	1 July	Grosvenor, G.	1866	20 Jan.	Streatfield, F. H. T.
1854	31 March	Harrison, W.	1866	28 June	Moran, G. R.
By 1855		Ford, R.	1869	8 Feb.	Oakley, C. S.
1855	18 June	Price, T.	1870	7 Sept.	Rawlinson, G. E.

Keeper and Assistant Keeper of the Criminal Register 1793–1860

The office of Keeper of the Criminal Register, which never formed part of the ordinary establishment, originated in 1793 when Raven began to receive, in addition to his salary of £80 as a Supplementary Clerk, an allowance of £70 a year 'for keeping a Criminal Register of the Felons in Newgate'.[1] This allowance, which was paid out of the contingent fund, was raised to £120 in 1795.[2] Raven's successor as Keeper, Day, was appointed at £50 in 1800, his allowance being raised to £80 in 1806.[3] In 1809 the office was brought within the terms of the order in council which provided increases of £80, £200, £300 and £400 after successive periods of five years' service.[4]

In 1828 an Assistant Keeper, S. Redgrave, was appointed with an allowance of £150, payable out of the contingent fund.[5] This was raised to £200 in 1830 while in 1836 provision was made for annual increases of £10.[6] In 1839 Redgrave was appointed a Junior Clerk on the establishment and his allowance as Assistant Keeper was reduced to £150.[7] In 1841 Day retired and, in accordance with a decision made in 1822, the office was regulated by order in council. Redgrave was appointed Keeper at £150 while retaining his position on the establishment. At the same time provision was made for an Assistant Keeper, to be chosen by the Keeper subject to the approval of the Secretary of State, with an allowance of £120.[8] This office was abolished in 1850.[9] In 1844 Redgrave's allowance as Keeper was raised to £300.[10]

The committee of 1856 recommended that Redgrave should be placed in charge of a new Police and Statistical Branch of the department and given the rank and salary of a Senior Clerk. The branch was formed at once and in 1858 Redgrave was given a consolidated salary of £880 rising after one year to £900.[11] In 1860 Redgrave retired and the Police and Statistical Branch was placed in the charge of a Senior Clerk on the ordinary establishment.[12]

---

[1] *16th Rept. on Finance*, 325; Nelson, *Home Office*, 61–2.

[2] HO 82/3, payments 17 Nov. 1795, 1 Feb. 1796.

[3] Ibid., payments 19 Jan. and 20 May 1801, 5 Nov. 1805, 4 Feb. 1806.

[4] Order in council 10 May 1809 (HO 45/9283/1782L); order of Earl of Liverpool 5 July 1809 (ibid.).

[5] HO 82/3, payment 5 April 1828.

[6] ibid., payments 5 July and 13 Oct. 1830, 5 Jan. and 5 April 1836, 5 Jan. 1837, 5 Jan. 1838, 5 Jan. 1839.

[7] HO 82/16; HO 82/83, payment 5 July 1839.

[8] Orders in council 28 March 1822 (HO 45/9283/1782L), 6 Oct. 1841 (ibid.).

[9] HO 82/2; T 13/3 pp. 324–5.

[10] HO 36/28 pp. 41–5; T 13/2 p. 132.

[11] HO 45/9483/1782M5; HO 45/9483/1782M5A; HO 36/32 pp. 374–8; T 13/5 pp. 221–2; HO 45/9483/1782M6A.

[12] T 13/5 pp. 348–9; T 1/6258A/13006.

LISTS OF APPOINTMENTS
KEEPER OF CRIMINAL REGISTER

1793	28 Sept.	Raven, E.	1841	6 Oct.	Redgrave, S.
1800	3 Aug.	Day, W.			

ASSISTANT KEEPER OF CRIMINAL REGISTER

1828	5 Jan.	Redgrave, S.	1847	5 April	Pyer, J.
1841	6 Oct.	Redgrave, A.	1848	May	Rowe, G.
1845	5 Jan.	Joseph, A. G.			

Clerk and Assistant Clerk for Criminal Business 1800–70

The Criminal Branch of the Home Office appears to have had its origin in the activities of Raven, a Supplementary Clerk, who also acted as Keeper of the Criminal Register.[1] From the date of his dismissal in 1800 another Supplementary Clerk, Capper, began to receive an allowance of £100 from the contingent fund for 'executing the Criminal Branch'. In addition to this allowance Capper continued to receive a salary of £70 as a Supplementary Clerk. In 1806 his total remuneration was fixed at £270.[2] In 1809 the post of Clerk for Criminal Business was brought within the terms of the order in council which provided increases of £80, £200, £300 and £400 after successive periods of five years' service.[3]

At some date before 1822 Capper acquired the assistance of a Supplementary Clerk, Trushard, whose allowance from the contingent fund, originally £260, was raised to £300 in 1824.[4] In 1822 it was provided that, on Trushard's departure from office, the position of his successor should be settled by order in council.[5] In the event no action was taken on Trushard's resignation in 1827, the work being entrusted not to a Clerk in the Home Office but to Everest, a Clerk on the Convict Hulk establishment which Capper superintended in addition to his duties as Clerk for Criminal Business. Everest's position was not regulated by order in council until 1845 when he was formally accorded the title of Assistant Clerk for Criminal Business and provided with a salary, payable out of Home Office funds, beginning at £300 and rising by annual increments of £15 to £400.[6]

On Capper's retirement in 1847 Everest succeeded him as Clerk with a salary of £550 rising by annual increments of £15 to £800.[7] In 1849 the salary scale was assimilated to that of a Senior Clerk on the ordinary establishment: £600 rising by annual increments of £20 to £800.[8] In 1860 the maximum was raised to £900 in accordance with the recommendation of the committee of 1856.[9] When the salary arrangements of the office were revised in 1866 Everest was again treated as a Senior Clerk and accorded a scale beginning at £700 and rising by annual increments of £25 to £1000.[10]

On Everest's promotion in 1847 the office of Assistant Clerk for Criminal Business was filled by a Supplementary Clerk, Joseph, with a salary of £150. This post lapsed in 1849 on Joseph's appointment as a Junior Clerk on the establishment.[11]

[1] See p. 25.
[2] HO 82/3, payments 24 Feb. and 11 Aug. 1801, 24 May and 1 Aug. 1806.
[3] Order in council 10 May 1809 (HO 45/9283/1782L); order of Earl of Liverpool 5 July 1809 (ibid.).
[4] HO 82/3, payments 11 April 1822, 7 July 1824, 10 July 1827.
[5] Order in council 28 March 1822 (HO 45/9283/1782L).
[6] Order in council 13 Jan. 1845 (HO 45/9283/1782G).
[7] Order in council 17 June 1847 (ibid.).
[8] Order in council 13 Feb. 1849 (HO 45/9283/1782L).
[9] T 13/5 pp. 340–1; T 1/6258A/13006.
[10] T 13/7 pp. 126–8; HO 36/35 p. 159.
[11] HO 82/2; HO 36/29 p. 412.

LISTS OF APPOINTMENTS

CLERK FOR CRIMINAL BUSINESS

1800	3 Aug.	Capper, J. H.
1847	17 June	Everest, G.

ASSISTANT CLERK FOR CRIMINAL BUSINESS

By 1822		Trushard, P.
1827		Everest, G.
1847	17 June	Joseph, A. G.

Clerk for Aliens Business 1836–49

This office was created in 1836 for the purpose of discharging the work formerly undertaken by the distinct Aliens Department. The salary scale was fixed at £300 rising by annual increments of £5 to £400.[1] The office was abolished in 1849.[2]

APPOINTMENT

1836   4 July   Kitching, J. F.

Clerk for Signet Business 1851–70

This post came into being in 1851 on the abolition of the offices of the Clerks of the Signet. The former Office Keeper to the Clerks was transferred to the Home Office in order to undertake certain residual functions connected with the Signet.[3] He gradually acquired other functions and was eventually designated Second Clerk in the branch for appointments and Clerk for Signet Business.[4] Originally the remuneration attached to the post was divided between a compensation allowance in respect of the holder's former office of Office Keeper of the Signet Office and a salary from the Home Office. The latter was fixed at £215 in 1851 and was raised to £350 in 1860. A consolidated salary of £600 was provided in 1866.[5]

APPOINTMENT

1851   5 Dec.   Sanders, H. W.

[1] T 13/1 p. 81.   [2] HO 36/29 pp. 384–5.
[3] 14 & 15 Vict., c 82, ss 3, 5; *Officials of the Secretaries of State*, 56–7; T 13/3 p. 287.
[4] HO 82/18.   [5] ibid.; T 13/5 pp. 269–70; T 1/6661B/19489.

Clerk for Roads Business 1853–70

This office had its origin in 1853 when three Clerks who had formerly been employed by the Surveyor of Roads were transferred to the Home Office. Two of these Clerks were henceforth ranked as ordinary Supplementary Clerks. The third, Morrish, was given a position of special responsibility and gradually acquired the title of Clerk for Roads Business or Clerk for Highways and Turnpike Trusts. The salary was originally £300.[1] In 1855 it was raised to £400 and a scale provided for future holders of the office beginning at £300 and rising by annual increments of £15 to £400.[2]

LIST OF APPOINTMENTS

| 1853 | 8 April | Morrish, W. J. |
| 1864 | 22 Oct. | Harrison, W. |

Clerks for Local Taxation Returns 1866–70

In 1860 the Home Office became responsible for the preparation of local taxation returns. At first their compilation was entrusted to law stationers' clerks employed on a temporary basis and paid out of a sum of £400 made available for the purpose. In 1866 the two Clerks so employed were given permanent status and a salary scale beginning at £150 and rising by annual increments of £10 to £300.[3]

LIST OF APPOINTMENTS

1866	Dec.	Ilett, T.
1866	Dec.	Buckingham, C. F.
1869	6 July	Collings, J. B. E. W.

[1] HO 36/31 pp. 34–5; T 1/13 p. 414. [2] HO 36/31 pp. 424–5, 452; T 13/6 pp. 451–2.
[3] 23 & 24 Vict., c 51, s 6; HO 36/35 pp. 296, 334–5, 357–8; T 13/7 pp. 273–4, 319; T 1/6661B/19489.

Librarian 1792–1865

This office originated in 1792, being placed on the establishment in 1822.[1] In 1849 the Librarian was given the additional title of Registrar.[2] The office was abolished in 1865.[3] The salary, originally £200, was raised to £300 in 1798.[4] In 1809 the office was brought within the terms of the order in council which provided increases of £80, £200, £300 and £400 after successive periods of five years' service.[5] Mills was appointed at a fixed salary of £600 in 1820.[6] In 1822 it was provided that, for future appointments, the scale should begin at £350 and rise by annual increments of £15 to £545.[7] In 1849 the scale was fixed at £450 rising by annual increments of £15 to £600.[8]

LIST OF APPOINTMENTS

1792	13 Oct.	Peace, C.
1806	15 May	Peace, W.
1820	5 April	Mills, F. R.
1849	1 April	Kitching, J. F.

Accountant 1868–70

This office was created in 1868. The salary scale was originally £150 rising by annual increments of £10 to £200.[9] In 1870 it was fixed at £250 rising to £400, for the first eight years by annual increments of £10 and thereafter by annual increments of £15.[10]

APPOINTMENT

1868   25 March   Pennefather, A. R.

[1] HO 82/3, payments 18 Nov. 1794, 1 June 1795; *16th Rept. on Finance*, 325; Nelson, *Home Office*, 60–1; order in council 28 March 1822 (HO 45/9283/1782L).
[2] Order in council 13 Feb. 1849 (HO 45/9283/1782L).
[3] HO 36/34 p. 482; T 1/6599B/18996.
[4] HO 82/3, payments 18 Nov. 1794, 1 June 1795, 6 Nov. 1798.
[5] Order in council 10 May 1809 (HO 45/9283/1782L); order of Earl of Liverpool 5 July 1809 (ibid.).
[6] HO 82/16.
[7] Order in council 28 March 1822 (HO 45/9283/1782L).
[8] Order in council 13 Feb. 1849 (ibid.).
[9] HO 43/112 p. 307.
[10] T 13/8 p. 443; T 1/7028A/22564.

Private Secretary to Secretary of State
1791–1870

The office of Private Secretary to the Secretary of State first acquired official standing in 1791 when a salary of £300, payable out of the contingent fund, was made available for its holder.[1] In 1795 the office was placed on the establishment.[2] Before 1830 the Private Secretaries were occasionally selected from amongst the Clerks on the establishment but from that year until the end of the period they were invariably appointed from outside the office. The payment of the salary was suspended in the case of Private Secretaries with seats in the Commons.[3]

LIST OF APPOINTMENTS

Dundas	1791–4	1791	8 June	Hepburn, R.
		1793	31 Dec.	Chapman, J.
Portland	1794–1801	1795	5 Jan.	Carter, T.
		1798	6 Aug.	Frankland, W.
Pelham	1801–3	1801	30 July	Fitzharris, Viscount
Yorke	1803–4	1803	17 Aug.	Edgcumbe, F.
Hawkesbury	1804–6	1804	12 May	Jenkinson, Hon. C. C. C.
		1804	6 July	Willimot, R.
Spencer	1806–7	1806	6 Feb.	Harrison, J.
		1806	19 March	Allen, Rev. J.
		1807	18 Jan.	Holland, H.
Hawkesbury/ Liverpool	1807–9	1807	25 March	Willimot, R.
Ryder	1809–12	1809	1 Nov.	Edgcumbe, F.
		1810	5 May	Peace, W.
Sidmouth	1812–22	1812	11 June	Peace, W.
		1812	26 Oct.	Inglis, R. H.
		1814	20 Feb.	Peace, W.
		1815	5 Jan.	Addington, Hon. W. L.
		1819	5 Jan.	Peace, W.
		1819	26 July	Mills, F. R.
		1820	24 April	Venables, T.
Peel	1822–7	1822	6 Feb.	Streatfield, S.
		1823	10 June	Venables, T.

[1] HO 82/3, payment 14 May 1795; Nelson, *Home Office*, 60.
[2] Order in council 27 Feb. 1795 (*16th Rept. on Finance*, 311).
[3] HO 82/16, case of Carter, Private Secretary to Portland, whose salary ceased 5 April 1796 on his election. This was probably also the case with Fitzharris (1802).

Sturges Bourne	1827	1827	30 April	Venables, T.
Lansdowne	1827–8	1827	16 July	Venables, T.
Peel	1828–30	1828	22 Jan.	Venables, T.
Melbourne	1830–4	1830	22 Nov.	Young, T.
Duncannon	1834	1834	19 July	Macdonald, N. H.
Wellington	1834	*No appointment traced*		
Goulburn	1834–5	1834	23 Dec.	Montagu, Hon. S. D.
Russell	1835–9	1835	18 April	Gore, C. A.
		1839	17 June	Russell, Lord E.
Normanby	1839–41	1839	2 Sept.	Yorke, P. J.
Graham	1841–6	1841	3 Sept.	Graham, G.
		1842	17 June	O'Brien, D.
		1844	2 Sept.	O'Brien, W.
		1844	1 Nov.	O'Brien, H. H. D.
Grey	1846–52	1846	July	Brand, H. B. W.
		1851		Baring, T. G.
Walpole	1852	1852	Feb.	Perceval, E. A.
Palmerston	1852–5	1852	Dec.	Grey, R. W.
		1854	May	Clifford, C. C.
Grey	1855–8	1855	Feb.	Ellice, R.
Walpole	1858–9	1858	Feb.	Perceval, E. A.
Sotheron Estcourt	1859	*No appointment traced*		
Lewis	1859–61	1859	June	Drummond, M.
		1860	May	Stephenson, B. C.
Grey	1861–6	1861	July	Loch, H. B.
		1863	Feb.	Waldegrave Leslie, Hon. G.
		1864	Oct.	Wood, C. L.
Walpole	1866–7	1866	July	Walpole, S.
Hardy	1867–8	1867	May	Perceval, E. A.
Bruce	1868	1868	Dec.	Rutson, A. O.

Private Secretary to Parliamentary Under Secretary 1865–70

While some Parliamentary Under Secretaries had the services of a Private Secretary at earlier periods, it was not until 1865 that the post was placed on the establishment with a salary of £150.[1] Its occupants do not occur in lists of the Home Office before 1870.[2]

APPOINTMENT

Knatchbull Hugessen	1868	By 1870	Stapleton, E. J.

Précis Writer 1791–1849

The Office of Précis Writer first acquired official standing in 1791 when a salary of £200, payable out of the contingent fund, was made available for its holder. The salary was raised to £300 in 1794.[3] The office was placed on the establishment in 1795.[4] It was abolished in 1849.[5]

LIST OF APPOINTMENTS

1791	8 June	Chapman, J.	1803	5 April	Shee, J.
1794	29 Sept.	Moss, R.	1804	14 Feb.	Manningham, H.
1801	30 July	Fitzharris, Viscount	1818	10 Oct.	Peace, W.
1803	5 Jan.	Byam, W.	1820	24 April	Mills, F. R.

[1] HC 90–II p. 7 (1865) xxxvi, 79. S. Redgrave had acted as Private Secretary to Maule (Aug. 1839–June 1841) and to Fitzroy (Dec. 1852–Jan. 1855) with an allowance of £150 out of the contingent fund (HO 45/9483/1782M8A).
[2] *Royal Kal.* (1870), 160.
[3] HO 82/3, payments 23 Aug. 1792, 3 Dec. 1794, 15 July 1795; Nelson, *Home Office*, 59–60.
[4] Order in council 27 Feb. 1795 (*16th Rept. on Finance*, 311).
[5] Order in council 13 Feb. 1849 (HO 45/9283/1782L).

Office Keepers 1782–1870

Two Office, or Chamber, Keepers were taken over by the Home Office from the former Southern Department. Until 1795 they received salaries of £20 16s each from the Secretary of State together with office fees and certain other perquisites.[1] In 1795 the salaries were fixed at £100 each.[2] In 1857 a scale was established beginning at £150 and rising by annual increments of £10 to £200.[3] In 1782 a Deputy Office Keeper, Crowder, was transferred to the Home Office from the former Colonial Office but he was not replaced on his death in 1784.

LIST OF APPOINTMENTS

1782	27 March	Kirby, W.	1821	5 April	Dyke, E.
1782	27 March	Doudiet, J.	1834	12 March	Sleeman, R.
1787	July	Gander, A.	1834	22 April	Taylor, W.
1788	July	Hancock, J.	1835	5 April	Forrest, R.
1806	5 Jan.	Ray, T.	1856	Aug.	Osborne, J.
1810	29 Nov.	Brown, T.	1862	March	Horton, J.
1813	5 Jan.	Smith, J.	1870		Priest, T.

[1] *1st Rept. on Fees*, 7, 24–5; Nelson, *Home Office*, 55–6.
[2] Order in council 27 Feb. 1795 (*16th Rept. on Finance*, 311).
[3] HO 82/18.

Housekeeper 1782–1862

The office of Housekeeper, or Necessary Woman as it was formerly designated, was taken over by the Home Office from the former Southern Department. Until 1795 the Housekeeper received a salary of £48 from the Secretary of State together with certain perquisites.[1] In 1795 the salary was fixed at £100.[2] In 1804 an additional allowance of £40 a year was provided.[3] In 1822 the salary was fixed at £140.[4] It was raised to £160 in 1826.[5] The office was abolished in 1862 when provision was made for the duties to be undertaken by the wife of one of the Office Keepers with an allowance of £50 a year.[6]

LIST OF APPOINTMENTS

1782	27 March	Emmitt, E.
1795	27 Feb.	Drinkwater, C.[7]
1797	11 May	Moss, A.
1821	5 Nov.	Allen, M.
1830	5 Jan.	Cook, E.

[1] *1st Rept. on Fees*, 7, 25; Nelson, *Home Office*, 56–7.
[2] Order in council 27 Feb. 1795 (*16th Rept. on Finance*, 311).
[3] HO 82/3, payment 1 May 1804.
[4] Order in council 28 March 1822 (HO 45/9283/1782L).
[5] HO 82/16.
[6] HO 82/18; T 13/6 p. 186.
[7] Acted as deputy Housekeeper 1782–95.

Office Porters 1782–1870

An Office Porter or Messenger was employed by the Home Office from 1782. At first he received no salary but was paid separate sums for each task that he performed.[1] In 1810 an allowance of £35 was provided.[2] By 1822 there were two Office Porters, one with a salary of £100 and an allowance of £50 for carrying letters and another with a salary of £85.[3] The salary of the junior Office Porter was raised to £95 in 1825. In 1838 the salaries were fixed at £110 and £85 for the senior and junior Porter respectively.[4] Between 1857 and 1860 a third Office Porter was employed and the number was fixed at four in 1865 when the grade was consolidated with that of Assistant Office Keeper.[5]

LIST OF APPOINTMENTS

1782	27 March	Henry, C.	1857	Webb, W.
1798		Woodlands, J.	1859	Haggard, S.
1821		Pinder, H.	1862	Burgess, R. H.
By 1822		Scutt, W.	1866	Baker, G.[6]
1835	5 July	Meyer, H. L.	1866	Keene, T.
1838	8 Feb.	Merritt, S.	1866	Gordon, J.
1845		Baker, G.	1870	Hockey, W. H.
1845		Burrows, C.		

[1] *1st Rept. on Fees*, 8, 21; *16th Rept. on Finance*, 322; Nelson, *Home Office*, 57.
[2] HO 82/3, payments 13 March and 17 April 1810.
[3] HO 82/3, payment 11 April 1822; order in council 28 March 1822 (HO 45/9283/1782L).
[4] HO 82/16.
[5] *Royal Kal.* (1858), 158; ibid. (1860), 159; ibid. (1866), 160; ibid. (1867), 160; HO 43/104 pp. 330–1.
[6] Re-appointed.

Door Porter 1810–70

This office came into existence in 1810. The salary, originally £110, was raised to £130 in 1822.[1] In 1835 it was reduced, in conformity with the order in council of 1822, to £100.[2]

LIST OF APPOINTMENTS

1810	8 Jan.	Youris, J.	1862	Haggard, S.
1810	8 Feb.	Mack, H.	1865	Webb, F.
1835	5 April	Loton, J.	1866	Priest, T.
1849	July	Osborne, J.	1870	Keene, T.
1856	Aug.	Collett, J. F.		

Assistant Office Keepers 1825–65

An Assistant Office Keeper was appointed in 1825 with a salary of £75.[3] A second Assistant Office Keeper was appointed in 1845 whose salary, originally £65, was raised to £75 in 1851.[4] In 1865 the title was discontinued, the then holders of the offices being thereafter classed as Office Porters.[5]

LIST OF APPOINTMENTS

1825	5 April	Williams, J.
1844		Collett, J. F.
1845		Baker, G.
1856		Webb, F.
1865		Priest, T.

[1] HO 82/3, payments 27 April and 12 July 1810, 6 July 1822; HO 82/16.
[2] Order in council 28 March 1822 (HO 45/9283/1782L); HO 82/16.
[3] HO 82/3, payment 5 July 1825.   [4] HO 82/18; HO 36/30 pp. 301–2.
[5] HO 43/104 pp. 330–1.

Counsel for Colonial Business 1782–1801

Before 1782 the task of reporting on the acts of colonial legislatures had been under-taken by a Counsel attached to the Board of Trade.[1] On the abolition of the Board in that year the responsibility for securing the necessary reports was transferred to the Home Secretary as the Secretary of State having charge of the colonies. The work was then carried on by a Counsel attached to the Home Office until 1801 when colonial business was entrusted to the Secretary of State for War who retained the services of Baldwin, the then Counsel. The Counsel was not paid a salary but received from the Treasury Solicitor a fee of three guineas for each report.[2]

LIST OF APPOINTMENTS

1782	July	Selwyn, W.
1783	April	Mansfield, J.
1783	Dec.	Selwyn, W.
1796	2 Feb.	Baldwin, W.

[1] *Officials of the Boards of Trade 1660–1870*, comp. J. C. Sainty (London 1974), 36–7. For the later history of this office, see D. M. Young, *The Colonial Office in the Early 19th Century* (London 1961), 58 n.

[2] TM 24 Feb. 1783 (T 29/53 p. 164); AO 3/1102; AO 3/1103.

Law Clerk 1791–1818

The post of Law Clerk was attached to the offices of the Secretaries of State between 1747 and 1774.[1] It was revived in 1791 within the Home Office with a salary of £300.[2] In 1795 the office was placed on the establishment.[3] During the period that it was held by Lamb it was a complete sinecure and it was discontinued on his death in 1818.[4]

LIST OF APPOINTMENTS

1791　1 Jan.　King, J.
1806　16 March　Lamb, T. D.

Counsel for Criminal Business 1796–1813

This office originated in 1796.[5] It was discontinued in 1813 on the death of Baldwin, its only holder.[6] The basic salary attached to the post was £500 but Baldwin received and additional £300 a year from 1796 until 1799 when he was appointed Receiver of the Police Offices.[7] In 1805 the salary, which had previously been paid at the Treasury, was made a charge on the Treasury Solicitor.[8]

APPOINTMENT

1796　23 Jan.　Baldwin, W.

[1] *Officials of the Secretaries of State*, 46.
[2] HO 82/3, payment 2 Jan. 1792; *16th Rept. on Finance*, 325; Nelson, *Home Office*, 59.
[3] Order in council 15 April 1795 (*16th Rept. on Finance*, 312).
[4] *Rept. of Select Committee on Sinecure Offices 1810* (HC 362 p. 11 (1810) ii, 601); HC 554 p. 6 (1822) xviii, 150.
[5] TM 7 March 1799 (T 29/74 p. 179); T 38/742 f. 60.
[6] AO 3/1103, payment 21 Dec. 1813; HC 554 p. 6 (1822) xviii, 150.
[7] TM 7 March 1799 (T 29/74 p. 179), 28 Nov. 1799 (T 29/75 p. 259), 28 July and 1 Dec. 1801 (T 29/78 pp. 39, 196); T 38/742 f. 101; order in council 27 Nov. 1799 (PC 2/153 p. 575).
[8] T 38/742 ff. 60, 85, 101; T 52/88 p. 35; AO 3/1103, payment 15 March 1805.

Parliamentary Counsel 1835–69

This office had its origin in the arrangements made by Peel, as Home Secretary, for the improvement and consolidation of the criminal law.[1] From 1824 a number of individuals were employed as parliamentary draftsmen at the expense of the government although none of them actually held a formal appointment. In the course of time their work was extended beyond the reform of the criminal law to the drafting of bills generally. In some cases payments were made in respect of particular bills.[2] However, from 1826 to 1833 William Gregson was employed on a continuous basis by successive Secretaries of State, receiving annual payments of £1000 from 1826 to 1828, £1260 in 1829, £1100 in 1830 and £1260 from 1831 to 1833.[3] From 1830 to 1833 he had an assistant, Henry Roscoe, at £500 a year.[4] Anthony Hammond, who was primarily concerned with consolidation, received a total of £3000 between 1825 and 1829.[5] Although these draftsmen worked under the direction of the Home Secretary they received their remuneration at the Treasury out of the funds provided for the expenses of the two Houses of Parliament.

Gregson's employment ceased in 1833 and he was not immediately replaced. For the next two years bills were prepared by a number of different draftsmen who received their remuneration from the Treasury Solicitor out of the money provided for law charges.[6] In 1835 Russell, as Home Secretary, obtained the approval of the Treasury for the appointment of a permanent Parliamentary Counsel whose salary was fixed in the following year at £1200.[7] In 1837 this office was formally incorporated into the establishment of the Home Office with a salary of £1500.[8] In 1842 its holder was made responsible for preparing bills for thirteen departments in addition to the Home Office and became, in effect, the principal government draftsman.[9] In 1848 the salary was raised to £2000.[10] The office was discontinued in 1869 when the then Counsel was appointed to the revived post of Parliamentary Counsel to the Treasury.[11]

---

[1] J. A. Gulland, 'The history of the criminal law reforms of the period of Peel's home secretaryship, 1822–1827', *Bull. Inst. Hist. Research*, viii (1930–1), 182–5; H. Parris, *Constitutional Bureaucracy* (London 1969), 174–7.

[2] T 38/14 p. 483; HO 36/21 pp. 348–9, 519.

[3] T 38/16 p. 294; T 38/17 pp. 7, 445; T 38/18 pp. 18, 570; T 38/19 p. 532; T 38/20 p. 171; T 29/344 p. 399.

[4] T 38/19 pp. 42, 532; T 38/20 p. 171; T 29/344 p. 399.

[5] T 38/15 p. 112; T 38/16 pp. 67, 477; T 38/17 p. 445; T 38/18 p. 112.

[6] HO 36/23 pp. 323, 328, 333–4, 334–5, 439–40; AO 3/1105.

[7] HO 36/23 pp. 450, 596; HO 36/24 pp. 64–5; T 13/1 pp. 36–7.

[8] HO 36/24 pp. 161–2; T 13/1 pp. 65, 91, 109; order in council 1 March 1837 (PC 2/219 p. 190).

[9] TM 18 March 1842 (HC 543, pt. ii pp. 170–2 (1847–8) xviii, pt. ii, 176–8); T 13/1 p. 378; *Rept. of Select Committee on Miscellaneous Expenditure* (HC 543, pt. i pp. 219–21, 307–11 (1847–8) xviii, pt. i, 283–5, 371–5).

[10] HO 36/29 p. 200; order in council 2 March 1848 (HO 45/9283/1782L).

[11] TM 8 Feb. 1869 (T 29/614 pp. 276–80); order in council 17 March 1869 (PC 2/269 p. 398).

LIST OF APPOINTMENTS

1835   28 Sept.   Drinkwater, J. E.
1848   2 March   Coulson, W.
1861   4 Feb.   Thring, H.

Clerks to Parliamentary Counsel 1836–69

Two Clerks were employed by the Parliamentary Counsel from 1836, the second of whom was regarded as temporary until 1838.[1] The salary, originally £78, was increased to £100 in 1843.[2] In 1851 it was provided that the salary of the senior Clerk should begin at £150 and increase by annual increments of £10 to £200 while that of the junior should begin at £100 and increase by annual increments of £10 to £150.[3] The offices ceased to exist in 1869 on the transfer of the Parliamentary Counsel to the Treasury.

LIST OF APPOINTMENTS

1836	10 Oct.	Fisk, R.
1836	10 Oct.	Parsons, E.
1840	5 April	Nichol, H.
1848	5 April	Morris, W.
1861	14 March	Godin, R.

Solicitor 1841–2

This office was created in February 1841 with a salary of £1500.[4] Its holder resigned in September of that year and was not replaced. The duties of the office were transferred to the Treasury Solicitor in 1842.[5]

APPOINTMENT

| 1841 | 2 Feb. | Vizard, W. |

[1] TM 5 May 1836 (T 29/377 pp. 119–20); HO 82/3, payment 5 July 1837; T 13/1 p. 177.
[2] HO 36/27 pp. 37–8; T 13/2 pp. 1, 12.
[3] HO 36/30 pp. 239–40; T 13/3 pp. 253–4.
[4] HO 36/26 pp. 51, 55–6, 148–9; T 13/1 pp. 297, 320.
[5] TM 18 March 1842 (HC 543, pt ii pp. 170–2 (1847–8) xviii, pt. ii, 176–8); T 13/1 p. 378; HO 36/26 p. 402.

Assistant on Irish Affairs 1867–70

This office had its origin in an arrangement, made in 1867, whereby an Irish barrister was transferred from the Irish government in Dublin to the Home Office for the purpose of dealing with questions arising out of the Fenian conspiracy. In 1868 the remuneration attached to the post was fixed at £50 a month.[1] Originally considered a temporary appointment, the office of Assistant had acquired a more or less permanent standing by 1870.[2]

APPOINTMENT

1867   17 Dec.   Anderson, R.

Legal Adviser 1869–70

This office was created in 1869 with a salary of £1000.[3]

APPOINTMENT

1869   30 Oct.   Lushington, G.

[1] HO 36/36 pp. 249–50, 432, 483; T 13/8 pp. 45–6, 169.
[2] HO 45/9283/1782MA5, postscript to report of 9 Dec. 1870.
[3] T 13/9 pp. 381, 386; T 1/6943A/21356.

Periodic List of Officials

LIST OF OFFICIALS ON THE FORMATION OF THE DEPARTMENT 27 MARCH 1782

Secretary of State
 Shelburne, Earl of
Under Secretaries
 Bell, J.
 Nepean, E.
Chief Clerk
 Shadwell, R.
Clerks
 Brietzcke, C.

Morin, J.
Randall, G.
Higden, W. H.
Carrington, G. W.
Daw, T.
Colleton, J. N.
Wilmot, E.
Chetwynd, Hon. R.
Palman, G. L.

Office Keepers
 Kirby, W.
 Doudiet, J.
Deputy Office Keeper
 Crowder, N.
Housekeeper
 Emmitt, E.
Office Porter
 Henry, C.

LIST OF OFFICIALS FOLLOWING REORGANISATION 28 MARCH 1822

Secretary of State
 Peel, R.
Under Secretaries
 Hobhouse, H.
 Dawson, G. R.
Chief Clerk
 Plasket, T. H.
Senior Clerks
 Hicks, J.
 Wood, R. R.
 Noble, T. H.
 Medley, R.
Assistant Clerks
 Norris, J. F.
 Venables, T.
 Walpole, F.
 Whish, H. F.

Junior Clerks
 Hoskins, G.
 Currie, F. J. G.
 Le Mesurier, T.
 Dawson, R. S.
 Knyvett, H. J.
Supplementary Clerk
 Redgrave, S.
Keeper of Criminal Register
 Day, W.
Clerk for Criminal Business
 Capper, J. H.
Assistant Clerk for Criminal Business
 Trushard, P.
Librarian
 Mills, F. R.

Private Secretary to Secretary of State
 Streatfield, S.
Précis Writer
 Mills, F. R.
Office Keepers
 Ray, T.
 Dyke, E.
Housekeeper
 Allen, M.
Office Porters
 Pinder, H.
 Scutt, W.
Door Porter
 Mack, H.

45

LIST OF OFFICIALS FOLLOWING REORGANISATION
13 FEBRUARY 1849

Secretary of State
Grey, Sir G.
Permanent Under Secretary
Waddington, H.
Parliamentary Under Secretary
Lewis, G. C.
Chief Clerk
Knyvett, H. J.
Senior Clerks
Currie, F. J. G.
Dawson, R. S.
Fitzgerald, C. R.
Leslie, F. S.
Assistant Clerks
Streatfield, J.
Erskine, C.
Redgrave, S.
Dillon, Hon. A. E. D.

Junior Clerks
Maling, H.
Gilly, F. D.
Joseph, A. G.
Maconochie, A.
Arbuthnot, R. C.
Supplementary Clerks
Dowling, R. H.
Playford, H.
Keeper of Criminal Register
Redgrave, S.
Assistant Keeper of Criminal Register
Rowe, G.
Clerk for Criminal Business
Everest, G.
Librarian
Kitching, J. H.
Private Secretary to Secretary of State
Brand, H. B. W.

Office Keepers
Taylor, W.
Forrest, R.
Housekeeper
Cook, E.
Office Porters
Merritt, S.
Burrows, C.
Door Porter
Loton, J.
Assistant Office Keepers
Collett, J. F.
Baker, G.
Parliamentary Counsel
Coulson, W.
Clerks to Parliamentary Counsel
Fisk, R.
Morris, W.

LIST OF OFFICIALS FOLLOWING REORGANISATION
25 JANUARY 1866

Secretary of State
Grey, Sir G.
Permanent Under Secretary
Waddington, H.
Parliamentary Under Secretary
Baring, Hon. T. G.
Chief Clerk
Fitzgerald, C. R.
Senior Clerks
Leslie, F. S.
Streatfield, J.
Erskine, C.
Dillon, Hon. A. E. D.
Assistant Clerks
Gilly, F. D.
Joseph, A. G.
Maconochie, A.
Arbuthnot, R. C.
Knyvett, C. J.
Hobhouse, E. A. S.

Murdoch, C. S.
Junior Clerks
Campbell, C. G.
Wharton, R.
Stapleton, E. J.
McClintock, F. R.
Defell, C.
Supplementary Clerks
Dowling, R. H.
Grosvenor, G.
Price, T.
Bentham, M. G.
Mills, F.
Cranston, R.
Streatfield, F. H. T.
Clerk for Criminal Business
Everest, G.
Clerk for Signet Business
Sanders, H. W.
Clerk for Roads Business
Harrison, W.

Private Secretary to Secretary of State
Wood, C. L.
Office Keepers
Osborne, J.
Horton, J.
Office Porters
Burrows, C.
Burgess, R. H.
Door Porter
Webb, F.
Assistant Office Keepers
Baker, G.
Priest, T.
Parliamentary Counsel
Thring, H.
Clerks to Parliamentary Counsel
Fisk, R.
Godin, R.

46

Alphabetical List of Officials

Adams, William Dacres   *Supernumerary Clerk* 17 May 1791–24 Oct. 1794 (HO 43/3 p. 257). *Clerk* 24 Oct. 1794–30 July 1810 (HO 43/6 p. 27). Res. 30 July 1810 on app. as Commissioner of Woods (HO 82/16; C 66/4104).

Addington, John Hiley   *Under Secretary* 20 Aug. 1812–22 April 1818 (HO 43/21 p. 138; HO 43/27 p. 253; HO 82/16).

Addington, Hon. William Leonard   *Private Secretary to Secretary of State* (Sidmouth) 5 Jan. 1815–5 Jan. 1819 (HO 82/16).

Allen, Rev. Joseph   *Private Secretary to Secretary of State* (Spencer) 19 March 1806–18 Jan. 1807 (HO 82/16).

Allen, Mary   *Housekeeper* 5 Nov. 1821–26 Dec. 1829 (HO 82/16). D. 26 Dec. 1829 (ibid.).

Anderson, Robert   *Assistant on Irish Affairs* 17 Dec. 1867 (HO 36/36 pp. 249–250).

Anstruther, Robert   *Junior Clerk* 5 Jan. 1829–30 Aug. 1847 (HO 82/16). Ret. 30 Aug. 1847 (HO 82/2; T 13/2 p. 321).

Arbuthnot, Robert Christopher   *Junior Clerk* April 1849–March 1860 (HO 45/9483/1782M17). *Assistant Clerk* March 1860 (HO 45/9483/1782M8C).

Baker, George   *Office Porter* 1845 (HO 82/2). *Assistant Office Keeper* probably app. 1845; occ. 22 Nov. 1851 (HO 36/30 pp. 301–2). *Office Porter* 1866 (HO 43/104 pp. 330–1; *Royal Kal.* (1867), 160).

Baldwin, William   *Counsel for Criminal Business* 23 Jan. 1796–10 Oct. 1813 (T 29/74 p. 179; T 29/78 p. 39). D. 10 Oct. 1813 (HO 36/17 p. 268).
   Counsel for Colonial Business 2 Feb. 1796–10 Oct. 1813 (HO 43/7 p. 364).

Baring, Thomas George (*styled* Hon. 4 Jan. 1866)   *Private Secretary to Secretary of State* (Grey) probably app. 1851; occ. 1852 (*Royal Kal.* (1852), 158). *Parliamentary Under Secretary* occ. from 23 April 1864 to 30 April 1866 (HO 43/101 p. 5; HO 43/106 pp. 364–5).

Beach *see* **Hicks Beach**

Beckett, John   *Under Secretary* 18 Feb. 1806–25 June 1817 (HO 43/15 p. 380; HO 82/16).

Bell, John   *Under Secretary* 27 March–April 1782 (HO 42/2, Bell's memorial, 28 Feb. 1783; SP 45/35, receipt for fees April 1782; Nelson, *Home Office*, 31).

Belmore, Somerset Richard (Lowry Corry) 4th Earl of *Parliamentary Under Secretary* app. 7 July 1866 (HO 43/107 flyleaf). Last occ. 19 July 1867 (HO 43/110 pp. 365–366).

Bentham, M.G.   *Supplementary Clerk* 9 July 1856 (HO 45/9483/1782M17).

Bernard, Scrope   *Under Secretary* 6 June 1789–23 Aug. 1792 (HO 43/3 p. 47; HO 82/3, payment to King 12 Nov. 1792; HO 88/2, receipts for fees Aug. 1792).

Bethune *see* **Drinkwater,** John Elliott

Bourne *see* **Sturges Bourne**

Bouverie *see* **Pleydell Bouverie**

Bradbury (from 21 March 1797 **Norton**), John *Clerk (Plantation Department)* Dec. 1783–9 Jan. 1789 (*1st Rept. on Fees*, 26). *Clerk* 9 Jan. 1789–8 May 1797 (HO 43/2 p. 348). Res. 8 May 1797 (HO 82/16).

Brand, Henry Bouverie William (*styled* Hon. 21 March 1851) *Private Secretary to Secretary of State* (Grey) July 1846–1851 (HO 82/2). Last occ. 1851 (*Royal Kal.* (1851), 158).

Brietzcke, Charles *Clerk* 27 March 1782–23 Oct. 1794 (HO 43/1 pp. 12–13; *1st Rept. on Fees*, 21). Ret. 23 Oct. 1794 (HO 43/5 p. 177; HO 36/8 pp. 413–14, 415).

Brietzcke, George Purchas *Clerk* 24 Oct. 1794–27 April 1817 (HO 43/6 p. 27). D. 27 April 1817 (HO 82/16; *Gent. Mag.* (1817), lxxxvii (1), 475).

Brodrick, Hon. Thomas *Under Secretary* 17 July 1794–13 Jan. 1795 (HO 43/5 p. 295). D. 13 Jan. 1795 (Burke, *Peerage*, under Midleton, Viscount).

Brown, Thomas *Office Keeper* 29 Nov. 1810–5 Jan. 1813 (HO 82/16). Left office 5 Jan. 1813 on app. as King's Messenger (ibid.).

Bruce, Henry Austin *Parliamentary Under Secretary* occ. from 21 Nov. 1862 to 18 April 1864 (HO 43/98 p. 116; HO 43/100 p. 416). *Secretary of State* 9 Dec. 1868 (*London Gazette* no. 23449; *Times*, 10 Dec. 1868).

Buckingham, Charles F. *Clerk for Local Taxation Returns* Dec. 1866–April 1869 (T 13/7 p. 319). Dis. April 1869 (T 13/8 p. 263).

Burgess, R. H. *Office Porter* probably app. 1862; occ. from 1863 to 1866 (*Royal Kal.* (1863), 159; ibid. (1866), 160).

Burrows, Charles *Office Porter* 1845 (HO 82/2).

Byam, William *Précis Writer* 5 Jan.–5 April 1803 (HO 82/16).

Campbell, Colin Glencairn *Junior Clerk* 1 Sept. 1856–Feb. 1868 (HO 43/89 p. 297). *Assistant Clerk* probably app. Feb. 1868 on increase in number of Assistant Clerks from seven to eight (T 13/7 pp. 541–2; HO 45/9483/1782M17).

Capper, John Henry *Supplementary Clerk* 20 April 1794–3 Aug. 1800 (HO 82/16). *Clerk for Criminal Business* 3 Aug. 1800–31 March 1847 (HO 82/3, payments 24 Feb. and 11 Aug. 1800). Ret. 31 March 1847 (T 13/2 p. 289).

Carew *see* **Pole Carew**

Carrington, George William *Clerk* 27 March 1782–23 Oct. 1794 (HO 43/1 pp. 12–13; *1st Rept. on Fees*, 22). Ret. 23 Oct. 1794 (HO 43/5 p.176; HO 36/8 pp. 413–414, 415).

Carter, Thomas *Private Secretary to Secretary of State* (Portland) pd. from 5 Jan. 1795 to 5 April 1796 (HO 82/16). Remained in office without salary after election as M.P. May 1796 (ibid.); probably left office 6 Aug. 1798 (*Royal Kal.* (1798), 104; app. of Frankland).

Chapman, James *Clerk* 7 July 1784–11 July 1794 (HO 43/1 p. 305). Left office 11 July 1794 on app. as Clerk, office of Secretary of State for War (HO 82/1; CO 324/107 p. 182).

    Précis Writer 8 June 1791–11 July 1794 (HO 82/3, payments 23 Aug. 1792 and 3 Dec. 1794).

    Private Secretary to Secretary of State (Dundas) 31 Dec. 1793–11 July 1794 (ibid., payments 8 July and 3 Dec. 1794).

Chapman, Robert *Clerk (Plantation Department)* probably app. Aug. 1786 in place of Porter; first occ. 1787 (*Royal Kal.* (1787), 104). *Clerk* 9 Jan. 1789–17 May 1791 (HO 43/2 p. 348). Res. 17 May 1791 (HO 43/3 p. 257).

Chetwynd, Hon. Richard *Clerk* 27 March 1782–25 Aug. 1786 (HO 43/1 pp. 12–13;

1st Rept. on Fees, 23). Res. 25 Aug. 1786 on app. as Clerk, Board of Trade (BT 5/4 p. 15; HO 43/2 p. 160).

Clerk, Sir George, 6th Bart. *Under Secretary* 5 Aug.–22 Nov. 1830 (HO 82/16).

Clifford, Charles Cavendish *Private Secretary to Secretary of State* (Palmerston) May 1854–Feb. 1855 (*Gent. Mag.* (1854), cxxxiv, 519).

Clive, George *Parliamentary Under Secretary* occ. from 23 June 1859 to 20 Nov. 1862 (HO 43/93 p. 236; HO 43/98 p. 116).

Clive, Henry *Under Secretary* 22 April 1818–18 Jan. 1822 (HO 43/27 p. 253; HO 43/31 p. 18; HO 82/16).

Colleton, James Nassau *Clerk* 27 March 1782–23 Oct. 1794 (HO 43/1 pp. 12–13; *1st Rept. on Fees*, 23). Ret. 23 Oct. 1794 (HO 43/5 pp. 177–8; HO 36/8 pp. 413–14, 415).

Collett, John F. *Assistant Office Keeper* 1844–56 (HO 82/2). *Door Porter* probably app. 1856; occ. from 1857 to 1862 (*Royal Kal.* (1857), 158; ibid. (1862), 159).

Collings, Joseph B. E. W. *Clerk for Local Taxation Returns* 6 July 1869 (T 1/6493A/21356).

Cook, Elizabeth *Housekeeper* 5 Jan. 1830–1862 (HO 82/16). Office abolished 1862 (T 13/6 p. 186; *Royal Kal.* (1862), 159; ibid. (1863), 159).

Coulson, Walter *Parliamentary Counsel* 2 March 1848–20 Nov. 1860 (PC 2/231 p. 173). D. 20 Nov. 1860 (*Gent. Mag.* (1861), cxlviii, 111).

Cowper, Hon. William Francis *Parliamentary Under Secretary* occ. from 7 March to 11 Aug. 1855 (HO 43/87 pp. 139, 404).

Cranston, Robert *Supplementary Clerk* 24 Dec. 1864 (HO 45/9483/1782M17).

Crowder, Nathaniel *Deputy Office Keeper* 27 March 1782–c. 12 Feb. 1784 (*Royal Kal.* (1783), 110; ibid. (1784), 103). D. by 12 Feb. 1784 (Prob. 11/1113 f. 68).

Currie, Francis John Gore *Clerk* 14 Aug. 1817–28 March 1822 (HO 43/26 p. 261). *Junior Clerk* 28 March 1822–23 Feb. 1827 (HO 82/16). *Assistant Clerk* 23 Feb. 1827–25 June 1837 (ibid.). *Senior Clerk* 25 June 1837–3 Nov. 1852 (ibid.). Ret. 3 Nov. 1852 (HO 36/30 p. 453).

Daw, Thomas *Clerk* 27 March 1782–8 May 1791 (HO 43/1 pp. 12–13; *1st Rept. on Fees*, 23). D. 8 May 1791 (HO 43/3 p. 257; HO 82/3, payment 18 July 1793 to Mrs. Daw).

Dawson, George Robert *Under Secretary* 18 Jan. 1822–30 April 1827 (HO 43/31 p. 18; HO 82/16).

Dawson, Robert Sharrock *Clerk* 5 July 1819–28 March 1822 (HO 43/28 p. 470). *Junior Clerk* 28 March 1822–10 July 1828 (HO 82/16). *Asistant Clerk* 10 July 1828–29 Aug. 1841 (ibid.). *Senior Clerk* 29 Aug. 1841–12 Aug. 1850 (ibid.). Ret. 12 Aug. 1850 (HO 36/30 p. 103).

Day, William *Keeper of Criminal Register* 3 Aug. 1800–29 Aug. 1841 (HO 82/3, payments 19 Jan. and 20 May 1801). Ret. 29 Aug. 1841 (HO 82/16; HC 137 p. 6 (1842) xxvi, 698).

Defell, Charles *Junior Clerk* 20 Nov. 1865 (HO 43/104 p. 303).

Dillon, Hon. Arthur Edmund Denis *Junior Clerk* 10 Feb. 1840–5 April 1849 (HO 82/16). *Assistant Clerk* probably app. 5 April 1849 in place of Leslie, Senior Clerk. *Senior Clerk* 1 Oct. 1865–1 Feb. 1869 (T 1/6599B/18996; *Royal Kal.* (1866), 160). Ret. 1 Feb. 1869 (HC o.3, vi p. 357 (1870) xlviii, 369).

Doudiet, John *Office Keeper* 27 March 1782–4 June 1787 (HO 88/1; HO 88/2; *1st Rept. on Fees*, 25). D. 4 June 1787 (*Gent. Mag.* (1787), lvii (1), 548).

Douglas, James Dundas *Clerk* 17 Feb. 1817–5 July 1819 (HO 43/25 p. 488). Left office 5 July 1819 (HO 43/28 p. 470; HO 82/16).

Douglas, Robert *Clerk* 17 May 1791–11 Nov. 1802 (HO 43/3 p. 257). Dis. 11 Nov. 1802 (HO 43/13 pp. 427–8).

Dowling, Richard H. *Supplementary Clerk* 6 Oct. 1845 (HO 82/4, payment 13 Feb. 1847; HO 45/9483/1782M17).

Drinkwater, Catherine *Deputy Housekeeper* app. c. 1783 (*1st Rept. on Fees*, 25). *Housekeeper* 27 Feb. 1795–10 May 1797 (*16th Rept. on Finance*, 309; HO 82/16). D. 10 May 1797 (HO 82/16).

Drinkwater (from 1837 **Drinkwater Bethune**), John Elliott *Parliamentary Counsel* 28 Sept. 1835–10 Feb. 1848 (HO 36/23 p. 450; PC 2/219 p. 190). Res. 10 Feb. 1848 on app. as Legislative Member, Supreme Council of India (PC 2/231 p. 173).

Drummond, Maurice *Private Secretary to Secretary of State* (Lewis) June 1859–May 1860 (*Times*, 22 June 1859).

Dunbar, William Cospatrick *Junior Clerk* 19 March 1869 (HO 43/114 p. 452).

Duncannon, John George (Brabazon) *styled* Viscount *Secretary of State* 19 July–17 Nov. 1834 (HO 82/16; *London Gazette* no. 19175).

Dundas, Henry *Secretary of State* 8 June 1791–11 July 1794 (*London Gazette* no. 13315).

Dyke, Edward *Office Keeper* 5 April 1821–12 March 1834 (HO 82/16). Left office 12 March 1834 (ibid.).

Edgcumbe, Frederick *Private Secretary to Secretary of State* (Yorke) 17 Aug. 1803–11 May 1804 (HO 82/16); (Ryder) 1 Nov. 1809–5 May 1810 (ibid.).
  Clerk 19 Oct. 1803–29 June 1811 (HO 43/14 p. 252). Res. 29 June 1811 on app. as Commissioner of Victualling (HO 43/19 p. 164; C 66/4112).

Ellice, Robert *Private Secretary to Secretary of State* (Grey) probably app. Feb. 1855; occ. from 1856 to 1858 (*Royal Kal.* (1856), 158; ibid. (1858), 158).

Elliott, Grey *Chief Clerk* (*Plantation Department*) Dec. 1783–18 Sept. 1784 (HO 36/4 pp. 13–18). *Under Secretary* (*Plantation Department*) 18 Sept. 1784–June 1787 (HO 43/1 p. 331). D. June 1787 (*Gent. Mag.* (1787), lvii (1), 548).

Emmitt, Elizabeth *Housekeeper* 27 March 1782–27 Feb. 1795 (*Royal Kal.* (1783), 110; *1st Rept. on Fees*, 25). Ret. 27 Feb. 1795 (*16th Rept. on Finance*, 309).

Erskine, Charles *Junior Clerk* 29 July 1834–5 Jan. 1849 (HO 82/16). *Assistant Clerk* 5 Jan. 1849–Nov. 1852 (ibid.; HO 36/29 pp. 385–9). *Senior Clerk* probably app. Nov. 1852 in place of Currie, ret.; first occ. 1854 (*Royal Kal.* (1854), 158).

Estcourt *see* **Sotheron Estcourt**

Everest, George *Assistant Clerk for Criminal Business* 1827–17 June 1847 (HO 45/9283/1782G). *Clerk for Criminal Business* 17 June 1847 (ibid.).

Fergusson, Sir James, 6th Bart. *Parliamentary Under Secretary* occ. from 1 Aug. 1867 to 27 Aug. 1868 (HO 43/111 p. 1; HO 43/113 pp. 370–1).

Finch Hatton, Edward *Under Secretary* 19 Feb.–18 Aug. 1801 (HO 43/12 p. 430; HO 43/13 p. 139; HO 82/16).

Fisk, F. *Clerk to Parliamentary Counsel* 10 Oct. 1836–8 Feb. 1869 (HO 82/3, payment 3 July 1837). Office abolished 8 Feb. 1869 (T 13/8 p. 185).

Fitzgerald, Charles Robert *Junior Clerk* 30 March 1823–23 May 1835 (HO 82/16). *Assistant Clerk* 23 May 1835–19 Feb. 1849 (ibid.). *Senior Clerk* 19 Feb. 1849–1 Oct. 1865 (ibid.; HO 36/29 pp. 385–9; HO 45/9483/1782M14). *Chief Clerk* 1 Oct.

1865–1 Nov. 1868 (HO 36/35 pp. 37–9, 41, 93). Ret. 1 Nov. 1868 (HO 36/36 pp. 398–9).

Fitzgerald, Gerald Beresford *Junior Clerk* 26 Nov. 1868 (HO 43/114 p. 165).

Fitzharris, James Edward (Harris) *styled* Viscount *Private Secretary to Secretary of State* (Pelham) app. 30 July 1801 (HO 82/16); pd. to 5 July 1802 (ibid.); probably remained in office without salary after election as M.P. July 1802 until Aug. 1803 when Pelham ceased to be Secretary of State.

  Précis Writer app. 30 July 1801 (ibid.); pd. to 5 July 1802 (ibid.); probably remained in office without salary after election as M.P. July 1802 until replaced by Byam 5 Jan. 1803.

Fitzroy, Hon. Henry *Parliamentary Under Secretary* occ. from 30 Dec. 1852 to 3 March 1855 (HO 43/82 pp. 3–4; HO 43/87 p. 136).

Ford, Richard *Supplementary Clerk* occ. from 5 Sept. 1855 to 26 Oct. 1865 (HO 45/9483/1782M4B; T 1/6599B/18996).

Forrest, Robert *Office Keeper* 5 April 1835–6 March 1862 (HO 82/16). D. 6 March 1862 (HO 82/4).

Frankland, William *Private Secretary to Secretary of State* (Portland) 6 Aug. 1798–30 July 1801 (HO 82/16).

Gaitskell, Henry *Supplementary Clerk* 21 March 1808–8 July 1811 (HO 82/3, flyleaf). Left office 8 July 1811 on app. as Under Clerk, Privy Council Office (PC 2/192 p. 275).

Gander, Anthony *Office Keeper* July 1787–28 Nov. 1810 (HO 88/2). D. 28 Nov. 1810 (HO 82/16; *Gent. Mag.* (1810), lxxx (2), 594).

Gilly, Frederick Dawson *Junior Clerk* 30 Aug. 1847–Nov. 1852 (HO 82/2; HO 82/16). *Assistant Clerk* probably app. Nov. 1852 in place of Erskine, Senior Clerk (HO 45/9483/1782M17).

Goddard, Charles *Clerk* 22 Aug. 1789–c. 24 Oct 1794 (HO 43/3 p. 78). Left office by 24 Oct. 1794 (*Royal Kal.* (1794), 104; HO 43/6 p. 27).

Godin, Robert *Clerk to Parliamentary Counsel* 14 March 1861–8 Feb. 1869 (HO 43/95 p. 308). Office abolished 8 Feb. 1869 (T 13/8 p. 185).

Gordon, Adam *Clerk* 17 May 1791–11 July 1794 (HO 43/3 p. 257). Left office 11 July 1794 on app. as Clerk, office of Secretary of State for War (HO 82/1; CO 324/107 pp. 120, 182).

Gordon, James *Office Porter* probably app. 1866; first occ. 1867 (*Royal Kal.* (1867), 160).

Gore, Charles Alexander (*styled* Hon. 8 Feb. 1837) *Private Secretary to Secretary of State* (Russell) 18 April 1835–17 June 1839 (HO 82/16). Left office 17 June 1839 on app. as Commissioner of Woods and Forests (ibid.; *London Gazette* no. 19743).

Goulburn, Henry *Under Secretary* 27 Feb. 1810–20 Aug. 1812 (HO 43/18 p. 87; HO 43/21 p. 138; HO 82/16). *Secretary of State* 15 Dec. 1834–18 April 1835 (HO 82/16; *London Gazette* no. 19221).

Graham, George *Private Secretary to Secretary of State* (Graham) 3 Sept. 1841–17 June 1842 (HO 82/2; HO 82/16). Left office 17 June 1842 on app. as Registrar of Births, Marriages and Deaths (*London Gazette* no. 20112).

Graham, Sir James Robert George, 2nd Bart. *Secretary of State* 3 Sept. 1841–6 July 1846 (HO 82/16; *London Gazette* no. 20014).

Graves, Alfred Percival *Junior Clerk* 4 Feb. 1870 (HO 45/9483/1782M17).

Gregson, William *Parliamentary Under Secretary* 3 Jan.–18 April 1835 (HO 82/16).

Grenville, William Wyndham (cr. Lord **Grenville** 25 Nov. 1790) *Secretary of State* 5 June 1789–8 June 1791 (T 52/78 pp. 218–19; *London Gazette* no. 13102).

Greville, Charles *Under Secretary* 14 March 1796–1 March 1798 (HO 43/7 p. 438; HO 43/10 p. 314; HO 82/16).

Grey, Sir George, 2nd Bart. *Secretary of State* 6 July 1846–27 Feb. 1852 (*London Gazette* no. 20620; *Times* 7 July 1846); 8 Feb. 1855–26 Feb. 1858 (*Times*, 9 Feb. 1855); 25 July 1861–6 July 1866 (*London Gazette* no. 22533; *Times*, 26 July 1861).

Grey, Ralph William *Private Secretary to Secretary of State* (Palmerston) Dec. 1852–May 1854 (*Gent. Mag.* (1853), cxxxii, 192). Left office May 1854 on election as M.P. (ibid. (1854), cxxxiv, 159).

Grosvenor, George *Supplementary Clerk* 1 July 1853 (HO 45/9483/1782M17).

Haggard, Samuel *Office Porter* 1859–62 (HO 43/102 p. 211). *Door Porter* probably app. 1862; first occ. 1863 (*Royal Kal.* (1863), 159). Left office Jan. 1865 on app. as Queen's Home Service Messenger (HO 43/102 p. 211; *Royal Kal.* (1866), 160).

Hancock, John *Office Keeper* July 1788–5 Jan. 1806 (HO 88/2). Ret. 5 Jan. 1806 (HO 82/16; HO 82/3, payments 5 Jan. 1806 and 3 Feb. 1809).

Hardy, Gathorne *Parliamentary Under Secretary* occ. from 3 March 1858 to 17 June 1859 (HO 43/91 p. 360; HO 43/93 p. 229). *Secretary of State* 17 May 1867–9 Dec. 1868 (*London Gazette* no. 23253; *Times*, 18 May 1867).

Harrison, John *Private Secretary to Secretary of State* (Spencer) 6 Feb.–18 March 1806 (HO 82/16).

Harrison, W. *Supplementary Clerk* 31 March 1854–22 Oct. 1864 (HO 36/31 pp. 244–5). *Clerk for Roads Business* 22 Oct. 1864 (T 13/6 pp. 451–2).

Hatton *see* **Finch Hatton**

Hawkesbury, Robert Bankes (Jenkinson) Lord (succ. as 2nd Earl of **Liverpool** 17 Dec. 1808) *Secretary of State* 11 May 1804–5 Feb. 1806 (HO 82/16); 25 March 1807–1 Nov. 1809 (ibid.; *London Gazette* no. 16014).

Headland, William John *Supplementary Clerk* 8 April 1853–18 June 1855 (HO 36/31 pp. 34–5). D. 18 June 1855 (ibid. pp. 428–9).

Henry, Charles *Office Porter* 27 March 1782–1798 (*1st Rept. on Fees*, 42). Last occ. 1798 (*Royal Kal.* (1798), 104).

Hepburn, Robert *Clerk* 6 Sept. 1786–9 Jan. 1789 (HO 43/2 p. 160). Res. 9 Jan. 1789 (ibid. p. 348). *Private Secretary to Secretary of State* (Dundas) 8 June 1791–31 Dec. 1793 (HO 82/3, payment 14 May 1795).

Hicks, John *Clerk* 24 Oct. 1794–28 March 1822 (HO 43/6 p. 27). *Senior Clerk* 28 March 1822–29 July 1834 (HO 82/16). Ret. 29 July 1834 (ibid.; HC 142 p. 5 (1835) xxxviii, 489).

Hicks Beach, Sir Michael Edward, 9th Bart. *Parliamentary Under Secretary* occ. from 29 Aug. to 14 Nov. 1868 (HO 43/113 pp. 378–9; HO 43/114 p. 147).

Higden, William Henry *Clerk* 27 March 1782–5 July 1805 (HO 43/1 pp. 12–13; *1st Rept. on Fees*, 22). Ret. 5 July 1805 (HO 82/16).

Hobhouse, Edward Augustus Stewart *Junior Clerk* Dec. 1854–Oct. 1865 (HO 45/9483/1782M17). *Assistant Clerk* probably app. Oct. 1865 in place of Dillon, Senior Clerk (ibid.).

Hobhouse, Henry *Under Secretary* 28 June 1817–31 July 1827 (HO 82/16).

Hockey, William H. *Office Porter* probably app. 1870; first occ. 1871 (*Royal Kal.* (1871), 160).

Holland, Henry *Private Secretary to Secretary of State* (Spencer) 18 Jan.–25 March 1807 (HO 82/16).

Horton, John *Office Keeper* probably app. March 1862 in place of Forrest; first occ. 1863 (*Royal Kal.* (1863), 159).

Hoskins, George *Clerk* 15 Feb. 1816–28 March 1822 (HO 43/24 p. 328). *Junior Clerk* 28 March 1822–24 March 1823 (HO 82/16). *Assistant Clerk* 24 March 1823–10 July 1828 (ibid.). D. 10 July 1828 (ibid.; *Gent. Mag.* (1828), xcviii (2), 92).

Howick, Henry George (Grey) *styled* Viscount *Parliamentary Under Secretary* 13 Jan.–23 July 1834 (HO 82/16).

Hugessen *see* **Knatchbull Hugessen**

Ilett, Thomas *Clerk for Local Taxation Returns* Dec. 1866 (T 13/7 p. 319).

Inglis, Robert Harry *Private Secretary to Secretary of State* (Sidmouth) 26 Oct. 1812–19 Feb. 1814 (HO 82/16).

Jenkinson, Hon. Charles Cecil Cope *Private Secretary to Secretary of State* (Hawkesbury) 12 May–5 July 1804 (HO 82/16). *Under Secretary* 30 Nov. 1807–1 Nov. 1809 (HO 43/16 p. 234; HO 82/16).

Jenkinson, Robert Henry *Clerk* 5 July 1805–24 Jan. 1817 (HO 43/15 p. 225). Res. 24 Jan. 1817 on app. as Receiver General of Stamp Duties (HO 82/16; HO 43/25 p. 488; C 66/4194).

Jessep, John *Clerk* (*Plantation Department*) Dec. 1783–9 Jan. 1789 (*1st Rept. on Fees*, 26). *Clerk* 9 Jan.–24 Aug. 1789 (HO 43/2 p. 348). Res. 22 Aug. 1789 (HO 43/3 p. 78).

Johnston, William Francis *Clerk* 24 Oct. 1794–7 Jan. 1799 (HO 43/6 p. 27). D. 7 Jan. 1799 (HO 82/16).

Jolliffe, Sir William George Hylton, 1st Bart. *Parliamentary Under Secretary* occ. from 28 Feb. to 24 Dec. 1852 (HO 43/80 p. 287; HO 43/81 p. 374).

Joseph, Allan Granville *Supplementary Clerk* 1 July 1839–5 Jan. 1845 (HO 82/3, payment 7 Oct. 1839). *Assistant Keeper of Criminal Register* 5 Jan. 1845–5 April 1847 (HO 82/2). *Assistant Clerk for Criminal Business* 17 June 1847–5 Jan. 1849 (ibid.). *Junior Clerk* 5 Jan. 1849–Feb. 1854 (HO 82/8; HO 82/16). *Assistant Clerk* probably app. Feb. 1854 in place of Maling, ret. (HO 45/9483/1782M17).

Keene, Thomas *Office Porter* probably app. 1866; first occ. 1867 (*Royal Kal.* (1867), 160). *Door Porter* probably app. 1870; first occ. 1871 (ibid. (1871), 160).

King, John *Law Clerk* 1 Jan. 1791–16 March 1806 (HO 82/3, payment 2 Jan. 1792). Res. 16 March 1806 (HO 82/16).
  Under Secretary 3 Dec. 1791–18 Feb. 1806 (HO 43/3 p. 327; HO 82/3, payment 12 Nov. 1792). Left office 18 Feb. 1806 on app. as Secretary, Treasury (HO 82/16; HO 43/15 p. 380; T 29/86 p. 113).

Kirby, William *Office Keeper* 27 March 1782–April 1788 (HO 88/1; *1st Rept. on Fees*, 25–6). Left office April 1788 (HO 88/2).

Kitching, Joseph Francis *Clerk for Aliens Business* 4 July 1836–1 April 1849 (T 13/1 p. 81). *Librarian and Registrar* 1 April 1849–30 June 1865 (HO 36/29 pp. 394–6). Ret. 30 June 1865 (HO 36/34 p. 491).

Knatchbull Hugessen, Edward Hugessen *Parliamentary Under Secretary* occ. from 5 May to 5 July 1866 (HO 43/106 p. 390; HO 43/107 flyleaf); reapp. Dec. 1868 (HO 43/114 p. 222; *Times*, 14 Dec. 1868).

Knyvett, Carey John *Junior Clerk* 9 Aug. 1852–June 1865 (HO 45/9483/1782M17). *Assistant Clerk* June 1865 (HO 45/9483/1782M13A).

Knyvett, Henry John *Clerk* 2 May 1820–28 March 1822 (HO 82/16). *Junior Clerk* 28 March 1822–29 July 1834 (ibid.). *Assistant Clerk* 29 July 1834–5 Jan. 1849 (ibid.). *Senior Clerk* 5 Jan.–5 April 1849 (ibid.; HO 82/2). *Chief Clerk* 5 April 1849–1 Oct. 1865 (ret. of Plasket; *Royal Kal.* (1850), 159). Ret. 1 Oct. 1865 (HO 36/35 pp. 33, 41; HO 45/9483/1782M14).

Lamb, Hon. George *Parliamentary Under Secretary* 22 Nov. 1830–2 Jan. 1834 (HO 82/16). D. 2 Jan. 1834 (ibid.; *Gent. Mag.* (1834), civ (1), 437).

Lamb, Thomas Davis *Law Clerk* 16 March 1806–13 May 1818 (HO 82/16). D. 13 May 1818 (ibid.; *Gent. Mag.* (1818), lxxxviii (1), 639).

Lansdowne, Henry (Petty Fitzmaurice) 3rd Marquess of *Secretary of State* 16 July 1827–22 Jan. 1828 (HO 82/16; *London Gazette* no. 18379).

Lefroy, George Thomson *Clerk* 24 Oct. 1794–9 July 1801 (HO 43/6 p. 27). D. 9 July 1801 (HO 82/16).

Le Marchant, Sir Denis, 1st Bart. *Parliamentary Under Secretary* 22 July 1847–15 May 1848 (HO 82/2).

Le Mesurier, Thomas *Clerk* 5 April 1819–28 March 1822 (HO 43/28 p. 340). *Junior Clerk* 28 March 1822–16 May 1826 (HO 82/16). D. 16 May 1826 (ibid.; *Gent. Mag.* (1826), xcvi (1), 574).

Leslie, Francis Seymour *Junior Clerk* 31 March 1827–25 June 1837 (HO 82/16). *Assistant Clerk* 25 June 1837–5 April 1849 (ibid.). *Senior Clerk* 5 April 1849–1 Nov. 1868 (in place of H. J. Knyvett, Chief Clerk; *Royal Kal.* (1850), 159). *Chief Clerk* 1 Nov. 1868 (in place of C. R. Fitzgerald, ret.; *Royal Kal.* (1869), 160).

Leslie *see also* **Waldegrave Leslie**

Lewis, George Cornewall (succ. as 2nd Bart. 22 Jan. 1855) *Parliamentary Under Secretary* app. 15 May 1848 (HO 82/2). Last occ. 8 July 1850 (HO 43/78 p. 147). *Secretary of State* 18 June 1859–25 July 1861 (*London Gazette* no. 22276; *Times*, 20 June 1859).

Liddell, Hon. Adolphus Freak Octavius *Permanent Under Secretary* 24 Aug. 1867 (HO 43/111 pp. 45, 117).

Lister, Charles *Junior Clerk* 23 May 1835–10 Feb. 1840 (HO 82/16). Left office 10 Feb. 1840 (ibid.).

Liverpool, Earl of *see* **Hawkesbury**, Lord

Loch, Henry Brougham *Private Secretary to Secretary of State* (Grey) probably app. July 1861; occ. from 1862 to 1863 (*Royal Kal.* (1862), 159; ibid. (1863), 159). Left office 14 Feb. 1863 on app. as Governor, Isle of Man (*London Gazette* no. 22708).

Loton, Joseph *Door Porter* 5 April 1835–c. 31 July 1849 (HO 82/16). D. c. 31 July 1849 (HO 36/29 p. 470).

Lushington, Godfrey *Legal Adviser* 30 Oct. 1869 (T 13/8 pp. 381, 386).

McClintock, Frederick Robert *Junior Clerk* 9 Aug. 1865 (HO 43/103 p. 270).

Macdonald, Norman Hilton *Private Secretary to Secretary of State* (Duncannon) 19 July–17 Nov. 1834 (HO 82/16).

Mack, Henry *Door Porter* 8 Feb. 1810–5 April 1835 (HO 82/3, payment 27 April 1810). Left office 5 April 1835 (HO 82/16).

Maconochie, Alexander *Supplementary Clerk* 12 March 1848–19 Feb. 1849 (HO 82/4, payments 5 April 1848 and 5 April 1849; HO 45/9483/1782M17). *Junior Clerk* 19 Feb. 1849–March 1860 (HO 82/2; HO 82/16, flyleaf). *Assistant Clerk* March 1860 (HO 45/9483/1782M8C).

Maling, Henry *Junior Clerk* 30 Aug. 1841–Aug. 1850 (HO 82/16). *Assistant Clerk* probably app. Aug. 1850 in place of J. Streatfield, Senior Clerk. Ret. 18 Feb. 1854 (HO 43/85 p. 47).

Manners Sutton, Hon. John Henry Thomas *Parliamentary Under Secretary* 3 Sept. 1841–July 1846 (HO 82/2; HO 82/16).

Manningham, Henry *Précis Writer* 14 Feb. 1804–10 Oct. 1818 (HO 82/16). Ret. 10 Oct. 1818 (ibid.).

Mansfield, James *Counsel for Colonial Business* April–Dec. 1783 (PRO 30/8/184 f. 54; T 29/56 pp. 116, 174–5; HO 36/4 p. 196).

Marchant *see* Le Marchant

Massey, William Nathaniel *Parliamentary Under Secretary* occ. from 16 Aug. 1855 to 24 Feb. 1858 (HO 43/87 p. 417; HO 43/91 p. 350).

Mathias, George Augustus Vincent *Clerk* 25 Feb. 1783–7 July 1784 (HO 43/1 p. 91). Res. 7 July 1784 (ibid. p. 305).

Maule, Hon. Fox *Parliamentary Under Secretary* 18 April 1835–15 June 1841 (HO 82/16).

Medley, Richard *Clerk* 22 Jan. 1799–28 March 1822 (HO 43/11 p. 47). *Senior Clerk* 28 March 1822–24 March 1823 (HO 82/16). Res. 24 March 1823 (ibid.).

Melbourne, William (Lamb) 2nd Viscount *Secretary of State* 22 Nov. 1830–19 July 1834 (HO 82/16; *London Gazette* no. 18748).

Merritt, Stephen *Office Porter* 8 Feb. 1838–1859 (HO 82/16). Last occ. 1859 (*Royal Kal.* (1859), 159).

Mesurier *see* Le Mesurier

Meyer, Henry L. *Office Porter* 5 July 1835–8 Feb. 1838 (HO 82/16). Left office 8 Feb. 1838 (ibid.).

Mills, Frederick *Supplementary Clerk* 10 Aug. 1859 (HO 45/9483/1782M17).

Mills, Frederick Russell *Clerk* 6 Feb. 1798–5 April 1820 (HO 43/10 p. 233). *Librarian* 5 April 1820–1 April 1849 (HO 82/16). Ret. 1 April 1849 (HO 36/29 pp. 394–6).
 Private Secretary to Secretary of State (Sidmouth) 26 July 1819–24 April 1820 (HO 82/16). *Précis Writer* 24 April 1820–1 April 1849 (ibid.; HO 36/29 pp. 394–6).

Mitford, Robert Sidney *Junior Clerk* 24 Feb. 1868 (HO 43/112 p. 223).

Montagu, Hon. Spencer Dudley *Private Secretary to Secretary of State* (Goulburn) 23 Dec. 1834–18 April 1835 (HO 82/16).

Montagu, William *Clerk* 10 Oct. 1810–15 Jan. 1815 (HO 43/18 pp. 345–6). D. 15 Jan. 1815 (HO 82/16; *Gent. Mag.* (1815), lxxxv (1), 182).

Moran, Gabriel Robinson *Supplementary Clerk* 28 June 1866 (HO 43/107 p. 152).

Morin, John *Clerk* 27 March 1782–23 Feb. 1783 (HO 43/1 pp. 12–13). Res. 23 Feb. 1783 (ibid. p. 91; HO 42/2 f. 100).

Morris, William *Clerk to Parliamentary Counsel* 5 April 1848–1 March 1861 (HO 82/4, payment 5 July 1848). Ret. 1 March 1861 (HO 43/95 p. 258).

Morrish, William John *Clerk for Roads Business* 8 April 1853–6 Aug. 1864 (HO 36/31 pp. 34–5). Ret. 6 Aug. 1864 (HO 36/34 p. 327).

Moss, Anne *Housekeeper* 11 May 1797–21 Oct. 1821 (HO 82/16). Left office 21 Oct. 1821 (ibid.).

Moss, Robert *Précis Writer* 29 Sept. 1794–17 June 1801 (HO 82/3, payment 1 June 1795; HO 82/16). D. 17 June 1801 (HO 82/16).

Murdoch, Charles Stewart *Junior Clerk* 5 Aug. 1856–Jan. 1866 (HO 43/89 p. 248). *Assistant Clerk* probably app. Jan. 1866 on increase in number of Assistant Clerks from six to seven (T 13/7 pp. 126–8; HO 36/35 p. 159; HO 45/9483/1782M17).

Nepean, Evan *Under Secretary* 1 April 1782–11 July 1794 (HO 43/1 p. 252). Left office 11 July 1794 on app. as Under Secretary, office of Secretary of State for War (CO 324/107 p. 2; app. of Brodrick).

Nichol, H. *Clerk to Parliamentary Counsel* 5 April 1840–5 April 1848 (HO 82/4, payment 5 July 1840). Left office 5 April 1848 (ibid., payment 5 April 1848).

Noble, Richard Hatt *Clerk* 7 Aug. 1797–28 March 1822 (HO 43/9 p. 514). *Senior Clerk* 28 March 1822–5 Jan. 1849 (HO 82/16). Ret. 5 Jan. 1849 (HO 82/2; HO 82/16; T 13/3 p. 18).

Normanby, Constantine Henry (Phipps) 1st Marquess of *Secretary of State* 2 Sept. 1839–3 Sept. 1841 (HO 82/16).

Norris, John Francis *Clerk* 10 July 1801–28 March 1822 (HO 43/13 p. 100). *Assistant Clerk* 28 March 1822–24 March 1823 (HO 82/16). *Senior Clerk* 24 March 1823–29 Aug. 1841 (ibid.). Ret. 29 Aug. 1841 (ibid.; HC 137 p. 6 (1842) xxvi, 698).

North, Frederick (North) *styled* Lord *Secretary of State* 2 April–19 Dec. 1783 (T 52/73 p. 55; *London Gazette* no. 12428).

North, Hon. George Augustus *Under Secretary* April–Dec. 1783 (HO 88/1).

Norton, *see* Bradbury

Noyes, Thomas Herbert *Junior Clerk* probably app. Aug. 1850 in place of Maling, Assistant Clerk; first occ. 1851 (*Royal Kal.* (1851), 158). Ret. 5 Feb. 1861 (HO 43/95 p. 223).

Oakley, C. S. *Supplementary Clerk* 8 Feb. 1869–c. 7 Sept. 1870 (HO 43/114 p. 325). Left office by 7 Sept. 1870 (app. of Rawlinson; HO 45/9483/1782M17).

O'Brien, Donatus *Private Secretary to Secretary of State* (Graham) 17 June 1842–2 Sept. 1844 (HO 82/2). Left office 2 Sept. 1844 on app. as Secretary of Railway Department, Board of Trade (ibid.; BT 5/52, 6 Aug. 1844).

O'Brien, Henry Higgins Donatus *Private Secretary to Secretary of State* (Graham) 1 Nov. 1844–July 1846 (HO 82/2).

O'Brien, William *Private Secretary to Secretary of State* (Graham) 2 Sept.–1 Nov. 1844 (HO 82/2).

O'Grady, Hon. Paget Standish *Junior Clerk* probably app. 9 Aug. 1852 at same time as C. J. Knyvett on increase in establishment (HO 36/30 pp. 409–10); occ. from 1853 to 1856 (*Royal Kal.* (1853), 158; ibid. (1856), 158).

Orde, Thomas *Under Secretary* April–15 July 1782 (Nelson, *Home Office*, 31; SP 45/35, receipt for fees May 1782; HO 43/1 pp. 12–13, 18).

Orr, James Stewart *Junior Clerk* 24 Feb. 1868–c. 4 Feb. 1870 (HO 43/112 p. 223). Res. by 4 Feb. 1870 (app. of Graves; HO 45/9483/1782M17).

Osborne, John *Door Porter* probably app. July 1849 in place of Loton; first occ. 1850 (*Royal Kal.* (1850), 159). *Office Keeper* probably app. Aug. 1856 in place of Taylor; occ. from 1857 to 1870 (ibid. (1857), 158; ibid. (1870), 160).

Palman, George Lewis *Clerk* 27 March 1782–23 Oct. 1794 (HO 43/1 pp. 12–13; *1st Rept. on Fees*, 24). Ret. 23 Oct. 1794 (HO 36/8 pp. 413–14, 415).

Palmerston, Henry John (Temple) 3rd Viscount *Secretary of State* 28 Dec. 1852–8 Feb. 1855 (*London Gazette* no. 21396; *Times*, 29 Dec. 1852).

Paradise, John *Supplementary Clerk* 8 April 1853–31 March 1854 (HO 36/31 pp. 34–5). Res. 31 March 1854 (ibid. pp. 244–5).

Parsons, E. *Clerk to Parliamentary Counsel* 10 Oct. 1836–5 April 1840 (HO 82/3, payment 5 July 1837). Left office 5 April 1840 (HO 82/4, payment 5 April 1840).

Peace, Charles *Librarian* 13 Oct. 1792–5 April 1806 (HO 82/3, payment 1 June 1795; *16th Rept. on Finance*, 325). Ret. 5 April 1806 (HO 82/16; HO 43/15 p. 472).

Peace, William *Supplementary Clerk* 25 March 1798–15 May 1806 (HO 82/16). *Librarian* 15 May 1806–24 April 1820 (HO 43/15 p. 472). Ret. 24 April 1820 (HO 82/16).

> *Private Secretary to Secretary of State* (Ryder) 5 May 1810–11 June 1812 (ibid.); (Sidmouth) 11 June–25 Oct. 1812 (ibid.); 20 Feb. 1814–5 Jan. 1815 (ibid.); 5 Jan.–26 July 1819 (ibid).

> *Précis Writer* 10 Oct. 1818–24 April 1820 (ibid.).

Peel, Robert (succ. as 2nd Bart. 3 May 1830) *Secretary of State* 17 Jan. 1822–30 April 1827 (HO 82/16; *London Gazette* no. 17783); 22 Jan. 1828–22 Nov. 1830 (HO 82/16; *London Gazette* no. 18436).

Peel, William Yates *Under Secretary* 22 Jan. 1828–31 July 1830 (HO 82/16).

Pelham, Thomas (Pelham) Lord *Secretary of State* 30 July 1801–17 Aug. 1803 (HO 82/16; *London Gazette* no. 15391).

Pennefather, Alfred R. *Accountant* 25 March 1868 (HO 43/112 p. 307).

Perceval, Ernest Augustus *Private Secretary to Secretary of State* (Walpole) probably app. Feb. 1852; occ. 1853 (sic) (*Royal Kal.* (1853), 158); probably app. Feb. 1858; occ. 1859 (ibid. (1859), 159); (Hardy) probably app. May 1867; occ. 1868 (ibid. (1868), 160).

Perceval, John Spencer *Junior Clerk* probably app. Nov. 1852 in place of Gilly, Assistant Clerk; occ. from 1854 to 1856 (*Royal Kal.* (1854), 158; ibid. (1856), 158). Last occ. 4 July 1856 (HO 43/89 p. 208).

Perceval, Spencer *Under Secretary* 30 April–16 July 1827 (HO 82/16).

Phillipps, Samuel March *Permanent Under Secretary* 31 July 1827–15 May 1848 (HO 82/16). Ret. 15 May 1848 (HO 82/2; HO 36/29 p. 242).

Pinder, Henry *Office Porter* probably app. 1821; first occ. 1822 (*Royal Kal.* (1822) 136; HO 82/3, payment 11 April 1822). Left office 5 July 1835 (HO 82/16).

Plasket, Thomas Henry *Clerk* 24 Oct. 1794–15 Feb. 1816 (HO 43/6 p. 27). *Chief Clerk* 15 Feb. 1816–5 April 1849 (HO 36/18 pp. 62–3, 64–5; HO 43/24 p. 328; HO 82/16). Ret. 5 April 1849 (HO 82/18; HC 171 p. 5 (1850) xxxiii, 647).

Playford, Henry *Supplementary Clerk* Aug. 1846–July 1852 (HO 36/30 p. 34). Ret. July 1852 (ibid. pp. 401–2).

Pleydell Bouverie, Hon. Edward *Parliamentary Under Secretary* occ. from 12 July 1850–19 Feb. 1852 (HO 43/78 p. 156; HO 43/80 p. 265).

Pole Carew, Reginald *Under Secretary* 17 Aug. 1803–29 May 1804 (HO 43/14 p. 146; HO 82/16).

Pollock, William *Chief Clerk* 1 June 1782–15 Feb. 1816 (ret. of Shadwell; HO 88/1; HO 43/1 pp. 12–13; *1st Rept. on Fees*, 19). Ret. 15 Feb. 1816 (HO 36/18 pp. 62–3; HO 43/24 p. 328).

Porter, John *Clerk (Plantation Department)* Dec. 1783–25 Aug. 1786 (*1st Rept. on Fees*, 26). Left office 25 Aug. 1786 on app. as Clerk, Board of Trade (BT 5/4 p.15).

Portland, William Henry (Cavendish Bentinck) 3rd Duke of *Secretary of State* 11 July 1794–July 30 1801 (HO 82/1; *London Gazette* no. 13682).

Price, Thomas *Supplementary Clerk* 18 June 1855–27 April 1869 (HO 36/31 pp. 428–9). Ret. 27 April 1869 (T 13/8 p. 270).

Priest, Thomas *Assistant Office Keeper* probably app. Feb. 1865 (HO 43/102 p. 279); occ. 1866 (*Royal Kal.* (1866), 160). *Door Porter* probably app. 1866; first occ. 1867 (ibid. (1867), 160). *Office Keeper* probably app. 1870; first occ. 1871 (ibid. (1871), 160).

Pyer, John *Assistant Keeper of Criminal Register* 5 April 1847–May 1848 (HO 82/2). Left office May 1848 (ibid.).

Randall, George *Clerk* 27 March 1782–16 Jan. 1798 (HO 43/1 pp. 12–13; *1st Rept. on Fees,* 22). D. 16 Jan. 1798 (HO 82/16).

Raven, Edward *Supplementary Clerk* 3 Feb. 1793–2 Aug. 1800 (HO 82/3, payment 7 May 1793). Dis. 2 Aug. 1800 (ibid., payment 22 Jan. 1801).
Keeper of Criminal Register 28 Sept. 1793–2 Aug. 1800 (ibid., payment 7 April 1794).

Rawlinson, G. E. *Supplementary Clerk* 7 Sept. 1870 (HO 45/9483/1782M17).

Ray, Thomas *Office Keeper* 5 Jan. 1806–5 April 1835 (HO 82/16). Left office 5 April 1835 (ibid.).

Redgrave, Alexander *Assistant Keeper of Criminal Register* 6 Oct. 1841–20 Dec. 1844 (HO 45/9283/1782L13; HO 82/2). Res. 20 Dec. 1844 on app. as Clerk, Factory Office (T 13/2 p. 126).

Redgrave, Samuel *Supplementary Clerk* 5 May 1818–5 Jan. 1828 (HO 45/9483/1782M8A). *Assistant Keeper of Criminal Register* 5 Jan. 1828–6 Oct. 1841 (HO 82/3, payment 5 April 1828). *Keeper of Criminal Register* 6 Oct. 1841–12 March 1860 (HO 45/9283/1782L13). Ret. 12 March 1860 (T 13/5 p. 348).
Junior Clerk 5 April 1839–19 Feb. 1849 (HO 82/16). *Assistant Clerk* 19 Feb. 1849–12 March 1860 (ibid.; HO 82/2).

Reynolds, John *Clerk* 19 Oct. 1803–25 Dec. 1805 (HO 43/14 p. 252). Res. 25 Dec. 1805 (HO 43/15 p. 336; HO 82/16).

Rice *see* **Spring Rice**

Rowe, George *Supplementary Clerk* 8 May 1845–May 1848 (HO 82/4, payment 5 July 1845). *Assistant Keeper of Criminal Register* May 1848–1850 (HO 82/2). Left office on app. as Junior Clerk, office of Receiver of Police (T 13/3 pp. 324–5).

Russell, Lord Edward *Private Secretary to Secretary of State* (Russell) 17 June–2 Sept. 1839 (HO 82/16). Left office 2 Sept. 1839 on app. as Private Secretary to Colonial Secretary (Russell) (ibid.; *Royal Kal.* (1840), 138).

Russell, Lord John *Secretary of State* 18 April 1835–2 Sept. 1839 (HO 82/16; *London Gazette* no. 19261).

Rutson, Albert Osliff *Private Secretary to Secretary of State* (Bruce) probably app. Dec. 1868; first occ. 1869 (*Royal Kal.* (1869), 160).

Ryder, Hon. Richard *Secretary of State* 1 Nov. 1809–11 June 1812 (HO 82/16; *London Gazette* no. 16311).

Sanders, Henry William *Clerk for Signet Business* 5 Dec. 1851 (T 13/3 p. 287).

Scutt, William *Office Porter* in office by 5 April 1822 (HO 82/3, payment 11 April 1822). Left office 1845 (HO 82/2).

Selwyn, William *Counsel for Colonial Business* probably app. July 1782 by T. Townshend, Secretary of State (PRO 30/8/184 f. 154; T 29/53 p. 164). Left office April 1783 (PRO 30/8/184 f. 154). Reapp. Dec. 1783 (ibid.; T 29/56 pp. 255, 410; HO 36/4 p. 244). Left office by 2 Feb. 1796 (app. of Baldwin).

Seymour, Edward Adolphus (Seymour) *styled* Lord *Parliamentary Under Secretary* 15 June–3 Sept. 1841 (HO 82/16).

Shadwell, Richard *Chief Clerk* 27 March–1 June 1782 (SP 45/35). Ret. 1 June 1782 (SP 44/330 p. 223).

Shee, Sir George, 1st Bart. *Under Secretary* 18 Aug. 1801–17 Aug. 1803 (HO 43/13 p. 139; HO 43/14 p. 146; HO 82/16).

Shee, John *Précis Writer* 5 April 1803–13 Feb. 1804 (HO 82/16). D. 13 Feb. 1804 (ibid.).

Shelburne, William (Petty) 2nd Earl of *Secretary of State* 27 March–10 July 1782 (*London Gazette* no. 12282).

Sidmouth, Henry (Addington) 1st Viscount *Secretary of State* 11 June 1812–17 Jan. 1822 (HO 82/16; *London Gazette* no. 16611).

Sleeman, Robert *Office Keeper* 12 March–22 April 1834 (HO 82/16). Left office 22 April 1834 (ibid.).

Smith, Jacob *Office Keeper* 5 Jan. 1813–5 April 1821 (HO 82/16). Left office 5 April 1821 (ibid.).

Smith, Wyndham *Junior Clerk* 25 June 1837–28 March 1839 (HO 82/16). Res. 28 March 1839 (ibid.).

Smyth, John Henry *Under Secretary* 27 July 1804–5 Feb. 1806 (HO 43/15 pp. 4, 367; HO 82/16).

Somerville, Sir William Meredyth, 5th Bart. *Parliamentary Under Secretary* July 1846–22 July 1847 (HO 82/2).

Sotheron Estcourt, Thomas Henry Sutton *Secretary of State* 3 March–18 June 1859 (*London Gazette* no. 22236; *Times,* 4 March 1859).

Spencer, George John (Spencer) 2nd Earl *Secretary of State* 5 Feb. 1806–25 March 1807 (HO 82/16; *London Gazette* no. 15887).

Spring Rice, Thomas *Under Secretary* 16 July 1827–22 Jan. 1828 (HO 82/16).

Stanley, Edward John *Parliamentary Under Secretary* 23 July–17 Nov. 1834 (HO 82/16).

Stapleton, Edward John *Junior Clerk* 9 Feb. 1861 (HO 43/95 p. 230).
  Private Secretary to Parliamentary Under Secretary (Knatchbull Hugessen) first occ. 1870 (*Royal Kal.* (1870), 160).

Stephenson, Benjamin Charles *Private Secretary to Secretary of State* (Lewis) May 1860–July 1861 (T 197/4 p. 80; *Royal Kal.* (1861), 159).

Strachey, Henry *Under Secretary* 15 July 1782–April 1783 (HO 43/1 p. 18; HO 88/1).

Streatfield, Edward *Junior Clerk* 8 June 1826–25 March 1828 (HO 82/16). D. 25 March 1828 (ibid.).

Streatfield, Frederick Henry Thomas *Supplementary Clerk* 20 Jan. 1866–1869 (HO 43/105 p. 241). Left office 1869 on app. as Clerk, Chief Clerk's Department, Foreign Office (*Royal Kal.* (1869), 160; ibid. (1870), 162).

Streatfield, John *Junior Clerk* 5 April 1828–29 Aug. 1841 (HO 82/16). *Assistant Clerk* 29 Aug. 1841–Aug. 1850 (ibid.). *Senior Clerk* probably app. Aug. 1850 in place of R. S. Dawson, ret.; first occ. 1851 (*Royal Kal.* (1851), 158).

Streatfield, Sidney *Private Secretary to Secretary of State* (Peel) 6 Feb. 1822–10 June 1823 (HO 82/16). D. 10 June 1823 (ibid.; *Gent. Mag.* (1823), xciii (1), 573).

Sturges Bourne, William *Secretary of State* 30 April–16 July 1827 (HO 82/16; *London Gazette* no. 18379).

Sutton *see* **Manners Sutton**

Sydney, Lord *see* **Townshend, Thomas**

Taylor, William *Office Keeper* 22 April 1834–1 Aug. 1856 (HO 82/16). Ret. 1 Aug. 1856 (HO 43/89 p. 269).

Temple, George (Nugent Temple Grenville) 3rd Earl *Secretary of State* 19–23 Dec. 1783 (*London Gazette* no. 12502).

Thring, Henry *Parliament Counsel* 4 Feb. 1861–8 Feb. 1869 (PC 2/253 p. 75). Left office 8 Feb. 1869 on app. as Parliamentary Counsel, Treasury (T 29/614 pp. 276–280).

Townshend, Hon. John Thomas *Under Secretary* 20 Feb. 1784–6 June 1789 (HO 43/1 p. 252). Left office 6 June 1789 (app. of Bernard; HO 88/1).

Townshend, Thomas (cr. Lord Sydney 6 March 1783) *Secretary of State* 10 July 1782–2 April 1783 (T 52/71 p. 400; *London Gazette* no. 12312); 23 Dec. 1783–5 June 1789 (T 52/73 p. 55; *London Gazette* no. 12503).

Trushard, P. *Supplementary Clerk* pd. from 7 Nov. 1808 to at least 10 Nov. 1810 (HO 82/3, payments 9 Aug. and 10 Nov. 1810). *Assistant Clerk for Criminal Business* in office by 1822 (orders in council 28 March 1822 (HO 45/9283/1782L) and 13 Jan. 1845 (HO 45/9283/1782G); HO 82/3, payment 11 April 1822). Ret. 5 July 1827 (HO 82/3, payments 5 and 10 July 1827).

Venables, Thomas *Clerk* 17 Aug. 1803–28 March 1822 (HO 43/14 p. 155). *Assistant Clerk* 28 March 1822–29 July 1834 (HO 82/16). *Senior Clerk* 29 July 1834–25 June 1837 (ibid.). D. 25 June 1837 (ibid.; Burke, *Landed Gentry* (1952), 2597).

Private Secretary to Secretary of State (Sidmouth) 24 April 1820–17 Jan. 1822 (HO 82/16); (Peel, Sturges Bourne, Lansdowne, Peel) 10 June 1823–22 Nov. 1830 (ibid.).

Vizard, William *Solicitor* 1 Feb.–Sept. 1841 (HO 36/26 pp. 148–9). Res. Sept 1841 (T 29/447 p. 381).

Waddington, Horatio *Permanent Under Secretary* 15 May 1848–14 Aug. 1867 (HO 82/2). Ret. 14 Aug. 1867 (HO 43/111 p. 117).

Waldegrave Leslie, Hon. George *Private Secretary to Secretary of State* (Grey) probably app. Feb. 1863 in place of Loch; occ. 1864 (*Royal Kal.* (1864), 159). Probably left office Oct. 1864 on election as M.P. (*London Gazette* no. 22900).

Walpole, Francis *Clerk* 29 June 1811–28 March 1822 (HO 43/19 p. 164). *Assistant Clerk* 28 March 1822–23 May 1835 (HO 82/16). *Senior Clerk* 23 May 1835–19 Feb. 1849 (ibid.). Ret. 19 Feb. 1849 (ibid.; HO 82/2; HO 36/29 pp. 363–4).

Walpole, Spencer *Private Secretary to Secretary of State* (Walpole) probably app. July 1866; occ. 1867 (*Royal Kal.* (1867), 160).

Walpole, Spencer Horatio *Secretary of State* 27 Feb.–28 Dec. 1852 (*London Gazette* no. 21296; *Times*, 28 Feb. 1852); 26 Feb. 1858–3 March 1859 (*London Gazette* no. 22103; *Times*, 27 Feb. 1858); 6 July 1866–17 May 1867 (*London Gazette* no. 23134; *Times*, 7 July 1866).

Webb, F. *Assistant Office Keeper* probably app. 1856; occ. from 1857 to 1865 (*Royal Kal.* (1857), 158; ibid. (1865), 159). *Door Porter* probably app. 1865; occ. 1866 (ibid. (1866), 160).

Webb, William *Office Porter* probably app. 1857; occ. from 1858 to 1860 (*Royal Kal.* (1858), 158; ibid. (1860), 159).

Wellington, Arthur (Wellesley) 1st Duke of *Secretary of State* 17 Nov.–15 Dec. 1834 (*London Gazette* no. 19211; *Times*, 18 Nov. 1834).

Wharton, Robert *Junior Clerk* 20 April 1860 (HO 45/9483/1782M17).

Whish, Henry Francis *Clerk* 2 Feb. 1815–28 March 1822 (HO 43/23 p. 460).

Assistant Clerk 28 March 1822–23 Feb. 1827 (HO 82/16). Ret. 23 Feb. 1827 (ibid.).

Wickham, William   *Under Secretary* 1 March 1798–5 Jan. 1801 (HO 43/10 p. 314; HO 43/12 p. 430; HO 82/16).

Williams, James   *Assistant Office Keeper* 5 April 1825–5 April 1844 (HO 82/3, payment 5 July 1825). Left office 5 April 1844 (HO 82/4, payment 5 April 1844).

Williams Wynn, Charles Watkin   *Under Secretary* 5 Feb. 1806–5 April 1807 (HO 43/15 p. 367; HO 82/16).

Willimot, Robert   *Private Secretary to Secretary of State* (Hawkesbury/Liverpool) 6 July 1804–5 Feb. 1806 (HO 82/16); 25 March 1807–1 Nov. 1809 (ibid.).
   Clerk 31 Dec. 1805–5 April 1819 (HO 43/15 p. 335). Res. 5 April 1819 on app. as Receiver General of Post Office (HO 82/16; C 66/4209).

Wilmot, Eardley   *Clerk* 27 March 1782–8 Aug. 1788 (HO 43/1 pp. 12–13; *1st Rept. on Fees*, 23). Ret. 8 Aug. 1788 (HO 36/6 pp. 124–6).

Wood, Charles Lindley (*styled* Hon. 21 Feb. 1866)   *Private Secretary to Secretary of State* (Grey) probably app. Oct. 1864 in place of Waldegrave Leslie; occ. from 1865 to 1866 (*Royal Kal.* (1865), 159; ibid. (1866), 160).

Wood, Edward   *Clerk* 24 Oct. 1794–22 May 1795 (HO 43/6 p. 27). Left office 22 May 1795 (ibid. p. 430; HO 82/16).

Wood, Richard Robert   *Clerk* 22 May 1795–28 March 1822 (HO 43/6 p. 430). *Senior Clerk* 28 March 1822–23 May 1835 (HO 82/16). Res. 23 May 1835 (ibid.).

Woodlands, John   *Office Porter* probably app. 1798; occ. from 1799 to 1821 (*Royal Kal.* (1799), 104—'Woods'; ibid. (1821), 136). Ret. 1821 (HO 82/3, payment 10 April 1822).

Wynn *see* Williams Wynn

Yorke, Charles Philip   *Secretary of State* 17 Aug. 1803–11 May 1804 (HO 82/16; *London Gazette* no. 15612).

Yorke, Philip James   *Private Secretary to Secretary of State* (Normanby) 2 Sept. 1839–3 Sept. 1841 (HO 82/16).

Young, Thomas   *Private Secretary to Secretary of State* (Melbourne) 22 Nov. 1830–19 July 1834 (HO 82/16).

Youris, John   *Door Porter* 8 Jan.–8 Feb. 1810 (HO 82/3, payment 27 April 1810). Left office 8 Feb. 1810 on app. as King's Messenger (HO 82/16).

Index of Offices